Hinduism is the oldest living religious tradition in the world. *Explore Hinduism* is a concise but well-rounded introduction to the variety of beliefs and practices, and describes how Hindus think, act and practice their faith in the modern world. Most importantly, it illuminates the 'soul' of Hinduism, its spirituality.

Bansi Pandit has an excellent grasp of the depth and breadth of Hinduism and his style is readable, making *Explore Hinduism* simple and undaunting for those approaching this religion for the first time.

Explore Books series editor: Bob Trubshaw

Other titles in the 'Explore' series include:

Explore Folklore Bob Trubshaw

Explore Mythology Bob Trubshaw

Explore Green Men Mercia MacDermott

Explore Shamanism Alby Stone

Explore Fairy Traditions Jeremy Harte

Explore Phantom Black Dogs edited by Bob Trubshaw

Forthcoming titles include:

Explore Dragons Richard Freeman

EXPLORE HINDUISM

Bansi Pandit

Heart of Albion

EXPLORE HINDUISM

Bansi Pandit

Cover illustration by Bob Trubshaw

ISBN 1 872883 81 8

Published by
Explore Books
an imprint of
Heart of Albion Press
2 Cross Hill Close, Wymeswold
Loughborough, LE12 6UJ

albion@indigogroup.co.uk

Visit our Web site: www.hoap.co.uk

Printed in England by Booksprint

Contents

List of figures and illustrations

Dates

Dates are shown as CE (for 'common era', traditionally referred to as Anno Domini or 'AD') and BCE (for 'before common era', traditionally referred to as 'Before Christ' or 'BC').

Acronyms and abbreviations

Ait-U	Aitareya Upanishad
AV	Atharvaveda (or Atharva Veda)
BG	Bhagavad Gita
Brh-U	Brhadaranyaka Upanishad
Chan-U	Chandogya Upanishad
Isa-U	Isa Upanishad
Kat-U	Katha Upanishad
Ken-U	Kena Upanishad
LOK	Law of Karma
Man-U	Mandukya Upanishad
Mun-U	Mundaka Upanishad
Pra-U	Prasna Upanishad
RV	Rigveda (or Rig Veda)
SV	Samaveda (or Sama Veda)
Tai-U	Taittiriya Upanishad
YV	Yajurveda (or Yajur Veda)

The digit proceeding the decimal point denotes the chapter. The digit before the comma (,) denotes the chapter or section. The digits after the comma denote verse numbers. Digits with a dash (–) between them denote the first and the last verse of the sequence.

Examples:

- Tai-U 4.2, 6–9 refers to chapter 4, section 2, and verses 6 to 9 of the Taittiriya Upanishad.

- BG 9,4 refers to chapter 9 verse 4 of the Bhagavad Gita.

Introduction

Hinduism is the oldest surviving religion in the world. No world civilization has been as continuous as that of the Hindus in India. While great civilizations of Egypt, Babylon and Assyria have come and gone, Hindu civilization has not only survived the onslaughts of time, but also is as vibrant today as ever before. One out of every six people on Earth today is a Hindu. The region where Hinduism originally developed was called Bharat (after the name of an ancient Hindu King, Bharat) which included what we now call India, Pakistan, Afghanistan, Nepal, Bhutan, Bangladesh, Burma, Sri Lanka, and parts of Tibet.

Hindus have received their religion through revelation, the Veda, which is the source book of Hindu tradition. Hindus maintain that the Veda is without beginning and without end. How can a book (or books) be without beginning or end? By the Veda, Hindus do not mean books. They mean the accumulated treasure of spiritual laws discovered by various people at different times in the course of the long history of Hindus and Hinduism in India.

The Vedas teach that creation is without beginning or end and appears in eternal cycles of creation and dissolution. Hindus believe that the soul of man (Sanskrit: *atman*) is eternal and immortal, perfect and infinite, and death means only a change of centre from one body to another. The present is determined by our past actions, and the future by the present. The soul will go on evolving up or reverting back from birth to birth and death to death, until it frees itself from material bondage. The Vedas teach that the soul will reach perfection when its material bond is broken, and the word they use for this phenomenon is moksha or *mukti* – spiritual freedom, i.e. freedom from the bonds of imperfection, death and misery. Thus the whole purpose of Hindu religion is to become perfect, to become divine, to reach God, and see God. This reaching God, seeing God, and becoming perfect – even as the Father in heaven is perfect – constitutes the religion of the Hindus.

On the surface, Hindu religion appears to be a religion of hopeless contradictions. On one hand, Hinduism teaches the highest spiritual philosophy of the Upanishads, complementary to the latest discoveries in science, and on the other hand, using the words of Swami

Vivekananda, it includes 'the low ideas of idolatry with its multifarious mythology.' On one hand, it includes pure theistic theology, and on the other, it embraces the agnosticism of Buddhists – Buddha is an incarnation of God in Hinduism – and atheism of the Jains. Where then is, one may ask, the centre of Hinduism to which all these divergent religious ideas finally converge? Or do they? This is a part of what this book shall attempt to explore.

Hinduism has the world's largest literature of yoga, meditation, timeless tales (mythology), spirituality and mysticism. It includes the world's largest tradition of goddess worship and is the world's largest pluralistic tradition, which recognizes one Truth, but many paths to realize it. It emphasizes spiritual experience over religious theories and theologies, book, dogma or saviour. Its religious insights are in harmony with modern principles of ecology and the New Age movement. There is a significant agreement between Hindu spirituality and modern science on critical issues such as the age of the universe, its evolution in eternal cycles, and the process of creation and dissolution. Carl Sagan, a twentieth century Cornell University scientist, calls the parallels between Hinduism and science 'astonishing coincidences.'

There is a profound contrast that persists between Hinduism and the West. The West has traditionally taken the anthropological approach whereas Hinduism represents a cosmic outlook. Saints and sages are its living heart. Hinduism's God is one invisible whole, which can be felt in the trees and stars, in the icons of gods and goddesses and experienced in the hearts of humans. Hinduism is a timeless tradition where the time dependent outer reality (physical world) is viewed only as a reflection of the timeless inner (spiritual) reality in the mirror of what Hindus call *maya* (cosmic ignorance), and where the divine presence is as close as the stillness behind our own thoughts.

Hinduism believes that the Divine Plan maintains the cosmic order and any infraction of the cosmic balance generates and implements the necessary correction in order to maintain the primal cosmic harmony and balance. Human action is a part of this divine plan. Hindu mythology is full of timeless tales to reflect this cosmic principle. Various aspects of Hinduism such as yoga, meditation, Ayurveda, Vedanta, and Vedic astrology are popular in the West today. Many gurus (spiritual teachers) of Hinduism such as Ramana Maharshi, Paramahamsa Ramakrishna, Parmahansa Yogananda, A.C. Bhaktivedanta Swami, Swami Shivananda, Maharshi Aurobindo,

Mahatma Gandhi and Amritanandamayi Ma have numerous followers in the West today.

Exploring Hinduism is thus an adventure, which will elevate your consciousness and expand your ideas of religion, spirituality and cosmic outlook. This book succinctly illustrates all the visible and tangible aspects of Hindu tradition: the scriptures, the Hindu view of God, the individual and the world, major doctrines and the important Hindu paradigms such as 'four-goals' and 'four-stages' models, rituals, symbolism and festivals. These are the 'heart' of Hindu religion. But more important are discussions illuminating the 'soul' of Hinduism, which is its spirituality.

Though there are numerous books available on Hindu religion, most of them are not suitable for beginners for exploring Hinduism. The language and writing styles of most of the books on Hinduism are too complex for beginners to comprehend. The purpose of this book is to assist readers of all ages in exploring Hinduism, and to provide them with a road map for further travels in the land of Hindu religion, if they so desire. Since the express purpose of this book is to present an overview of Hindu religious and spiritual thought in an easily understandable format, a serious effort has been made to provide the material in a logical manner and to keep the language simple and straightforward. Basic concepts are stressed with the hope that once readers have acquired an understanding of the fundamentals of Hindu religion and spirituality, they can proceed on their own to gain a better understanding of the higher teachings contained in other books. Accordingly, this book includes the following features:

The book is divided into two parts. The first part discusses all essential aspects of Hindu religion and culture. The second part covers the fundamentals of Hindu spirituality, including the attributes of a spiritual *sadhana* (path). To broaden the reader's understanding of the material presented, the book also includes tables, figures, glossary, bibliography and index. The figures are included with their respective chapters.

Each chapter is essentially self-contained and can be read independently of the others. Cross-references to other sections of the book have been provided in each chapter for a more comprehensive understanding of the contents. Whenever a Sanskrit word initially appears in a chapter, the English translation is provided in parenthesis. However, the meanings of many Sanskrit words cannot possibly be conveyed through simple, one-word translations. To this extent, a glossary is also provided.

The author sincerely hopes that this engaging overview will greatly assist you to explore the landscape of Hinduism. It will challenge, expand, and transform your view of the Hindu religion, culture and spirituality.

Glen Ellyn, Illinois

August 2005

Chapter 1

The Nature and Origin of Hinduism

Over a billion Hindus, mostly living in India, practice Hinduism, the oldest living religious tradition in the world. Large populations of Hindus also live in other countries including Bangladesh, Bhutan, Canada, Fiji, Guyana, Indonesia, Mauritius, Nepal, Pakistan, South Africa, Sri Lanka, Trinidad, United Kingdom and USA.

Hinduism is not a religion that is immediately evident and understandable because of its enormous diversity and variety. It presents a significant challenge to convert its wide-ranging theology into a set of codes and commandments. The religious, spiritual, social, and cultural patterns of Hinduism are the product of theories and theologies, which are significantly different from those of the other religions of the world.

Hinduism does not constitute a single system of religious thought, as it was not founded by one prophet, saviour, or incarnation of God. It is an ethnic and not a creedal tradition. As such, it is closely associated with the people of India, their history, mythology, folklore, social customs and manners. Hinduism consists of universal laws, which govern the human as well as non-human existence. Hinduism is to human life what natural laws are to the physical phenomena. Just as the phenomena of gravity existed before it was discovered, the spiritual laws of life existed before they were discovered by the ancient *rishis* (sages) of India for humanity. The very name Hinduism does not exist in Hindu scriptures. In ancient times, the people living on the banks of river Indus (*Sindh* in Sanskrit), in the north-western region of present day India, were called *Sindhus* by Persians. In the language of the Persians, the word *Sindhu* became *Hindu* and the people living in ancient India came to be known as Hindus and their religion as Hinduism. The original name of Hinduism, as it exists in Hindu scriptures, is *Sanatana Dharma*, meaning 'eternal or universal religion or righteousness'.

Hinduism maintains that the ultimate reality, the ground of infinite potentiality and actualization, cannot be limited by any one name, thought or concept. Hindus maintain that the potential for transformation of human consciousness into divine consciousness (or in other frames of reference, enlightenment, salvation, liberation, transformation, blessedness, *nirvana* and *moksha*) is present in every human being. No race or religion is superior or inferior. All humans are spiritually united like drops of water in an ocean.

Hinduism does not enforce one belief, one way of worship or one code of conduct for all its followers. It considers such enforcement of uniformity to be unnatural and contrary to the divine law, as it limits freedom of thought and hinders progress of individuals in their journey to the state of divinity, which is the supreme goal of Hindu religious tradition.

Hinduism emphasizes sincerity of heart and nobleness of conduct in the field of religion. It provides freedom to think, freedom to believe, freedom to disbelieve and freedom to adopt a way of worship, which suits one's temperament. Hinduism believes that what is important in worship of God is sincerity of the heart and not the outer form of worship.

Hinduism may be better understood by recognizing what is not Hinduism rather than what is Hinduism. It is often said that there are more religious traditions inside Hinduism than outside it. Hinduism may be called the mother of religions, as it includes numerous philosophies and theologies and is based upon actual spiritual experiences and insights of many ancient, medieval, and modern sages and seers, giving rise to a variety of religious beliefs and practices, which form the basis for diverse types of religious life in Hinduism. To a Hindu, every tradition, which helps to elevate one's consciousness to God, is considered valid and worthy of adherence.

Hinduism is not simply a system of ethics or theology, though it includes the most comprehensive code of ethics man has ever devised, and more than one complete school of theology. Hinduism is essentially a school of metaphysics and its aim is not only to make people perfect human beings on Earth and/or reward them in heaven, but to make them, in this very life, one with the ultimate reality, the eternal spirit residing in the heart of every creature. Thus, the ultimate goal of Hindu religious life is to transform human consciousness into divine consciousness. This goal cannot be reached merely by improving human conduct or reforming human character, but by living a spiritual life that includes not only an ethical and moral discipline, but also a *sadhana* (spiritual discipline) that transforms one's consciousness.

Hinduism is the repository of the world's largest literature of spirituality, mysticism and spiritual culture. Hinduism does not confine itself only to religious doctrines; it considers political and social philosophy, art, science and technology as expressions of the same divine spirit that is present in every creature. Thus, Hindu political and social institutions and their arts and sciences are not ends in themselves, but the means to elevate human consciousness to make it one with the ultimate reality, called *brahman*.

Origin of Hinduism

An ancient civilization, popularly known as the Harappan civilization (sometimes called Indus or Indus Saraswati civilization) existed in the third millennium BCE in the north-western region of India, by the rivers Indus and Saraswati (the latter dried up in 1900 BCE). Nothing of this civilization was known until the early part of the twentieth century, when Indian archaeologists discovered Mohenjodaro and Harappan sites in 1920–22. About 200 additional sites have now been excavated on a large scale. The archaeological remains show that the Harappan Civilization was a highly developed one, covering an area of over 700 miles from north to south and 800 miles east to west. The towns were planned with roads running north-south and east-west, and intersecting at right angles. The houses were built of bricks and stones with stairs, bathrooms and well-designed drainage systems. The widely discussed tank at Mohenjodaro, called the Great Bath, is an engineering marvel of these times. It shows an amazing perfection in building techniques. The tank is 39 feet long, 23 feet wide, and 8 feet deep with an opening in one corner for drainage. It was made watertight by using fired bricks held together with lime and asphalt. These people had pots made of baked clay, gold and silver jewellery and a variety of clay toys, stone and terracotta seals and figurines. They used ploughs to till the land and grew crops including wheat, pulses, barley, cotton, millet, dates and other fruits.

The religious life of these ancient people was vibrant. The archaeological evidence shows that the ancients worshipped Pashupati (the forerunner of the present Hindu deity Shiva) as the male aspect and the Mother Goddess as the female aspect of the Divine. Pashupati was also assigned the role of an ascetic (*Mahayogi*) and is shown sitting cross-legged in deep meditation (see Figure 1). This evidence demonstrates that Hindu religion was practised in one form or the other in the Harappan culture that reached its peak around 3000 BCE.

Above: *Pashupati or Proto-Shiva seal, 2700 BC. Steatite, Mohoenjodaro. This unique seal depicts Shiva seated in a yogic posture. He has three faces and is surrounded by animals and a man.* Opposite: *Pashupati Shiva figure (head) pained on a storage jar from Padri (Gujaret, India), 2800 BC.*
(Both photos courtesy of National Museum, New Delhi, India.)

The origin of Hinduism is buried in the archives of human history. The exact time and place of its origin is impossible to pinpoint, since it is a prehistoric tradition and the most ancient writings neglect the chronology and authorship. Hindu scriptures such as the *Puranas* and the *Mahabharata* often mention legendary kings and heroes of the ancient cities and provide conclusive evidence that Hindu tradition is over 10,000 years old and that India was the original homeland of the Indo-European family of languages. The Rigveda, the oldest religious literature of the human race, mentions stellar configurations that occurred between 6000 to 7000 BCE. It often talks about the river

Saraswati, which according to the current archaeological findings, dried up around 1900 BCE. By these accounts, Hinduism is at least eight to ten thousand years old. However, if we look at the encyclopaedias and majority of books written by Western authors, we are told that the Vedic religion, precursor of the contemporary Hinduism, was established in 1200 BCE by Aryans, who invaded India in 1500 BCE and spread their Vedic culture in India thereafter. Why is the Western version of Hindu history different from the Hindu version of Hindu history?

Mother Goddess, 2700–2100 BC, Mohenjodaro. (Photo courtesy of National Museum, New Delhi, India.)

Western scholars did not believe the Hindu view of the universe, according to which the universe appears in cycles and that the present cycle is billions of years old. The major voice of the Western scholars in the nineteenth century was the Oxford University professor Frederick Max Müller, who put forth a theory that came to be known as the Aryan Invasion Theory. The nineteenth century European scholars accepted this theory, since Professor Müller was held in high esteem by Western scholars of the time. According to the Aryan Invasion Theory, hordes of semi-barbarian, pastoral nomads, the so-called *Aryans* poured out of Central Asia into the north-western region of India, and drove the original inhabitants, the Dravidians, to the southern region of India. The invading Aryans subsequently composed the Vedas over a few centuries and gradually spread their Vedic culture, the forerunner of the present-day Hinduism, all over India. Why did Müller ignore the historical accounts of Hindu scriptures and put forth his own theory?

Müller was a devout Christian and believed in the Biblical chronology, according to which the world was created in 4000 BCE. This led him to conclude that nothing could have existed before this date and, thus the Vedas had to be of a later date. He treated the historical accounts in the Vedas and other Hindu scriptures as mythical and ignored them completely. Based upon the ages of the patriarchs listed in the Bible, Müller calculated that approximately 1500 years had passed since the creation of the world and the Great Deluge. Allowing approximately another 1300 years for Aryans (perhaps Noah's descendants) to arrive in India and develop different languages and culture, he put forth 1200 BCE (4000 less 1500 less 1300) as the earliest date for composition of the Rigveda, the oldest of the four Vedas. This is why to this day the majority of books written by Western scholars still show 1200 BCE as the date of composition of the Vedas and the beginning of Hinduism.

The modern archaeological and literary evidence invalidates the Aryan Invasion Theory and proves that Hindus had been correct all along in formulating their own history. There is plenty of the archaeological and literary evidence available now to show that India was the original homeland of the Aryans or Indo-European languages. The current evidence suggests that the Indo-Aryans were present in India as an ethnic sub-group of the Vedic people before 6500 BCE and the famous Harappan culture was a continuation of the Vedic culture.

The Vedic Period (6500 BCE or earlier, to 500 BCE)

The authoritative literature of Hinduism consists of the four sacred books (called Vedas – see Chapter 2). Each Veda comprises four parts: *Mantras, Brahmanas, Arnyakas,* and *Upanishads.* The *Mantras* were compiled to praise and worship the forces of nature, such as fire, wind and rain. In the beginning, there was no clear demarcation between one Vedic deity and another, since all represented creative powers of nature. In the earlier times, two of the Vedic deities rose to prominence: Indra, the deity of power, and Varuna, the deity of righteousness. Additional deities such as Prajapati (lord of the creatures), Aditi (the infinite), Prana (life) and Kala (time) were added to further personify the forces of nature. Two major developments took place during this period. First, the amazing march of the human mind from the worship of the forces of nature to the conception of the cosmic absolute, which was fully developed later in the Upanishads. Second, the conception of *Rita,* the cosmic order, from which were developed later the doctrine of *dharma* and *karma* (see Chapters 7 and 8).

During the earliest stages, *Rita* was conceived only as natural order, such as movements of the heavenly bodies and succession of the seasons. Soon *Rita* was recognized as both the moral as well as the natural order. Deities were considered as guardians of the moral and natural order and had to be propitiated by means of religious rites and rituals. This gave rise to the practice of the Vedic sacrifices, which were considered necessary for maintenance of the natural and moral order. This idea led to a professional class of priests who were required to conduct the sacrifices correctly along with chanting of the *mantras* (sacred verses).

The period of the *Mantras* was followed by the period of the *Brahmanas* (2000–1000 BCE). During this period the, doctrines of the four stages of life (*varna, ashrama, dharma*) were developed (see Chapter 10). Prajapati rose to the prominence and was worshipped as chief deity and the creator. Vishnu became the deity to preside over sacrifices and Shiva (a pre-Vedic deity) became identified with the Vedic deity, Rudra. The priesthood became all-powerful and congregational sacrifices were conducted on a large scale.

The age of the *Brahmanas* was followed by the age of the *Aranyakas* and finally the *Upanishads* (1000–500 BCE). If the *Mantras* and the *Brahmanas* were the age of the priests, the *Aranyakas* and the *Upanishads* were the age of the prophets. The *Upanishads* are the soul of Hindu spiritual thought. They are considered authoritative by all traditions (*sampradayas*) of Hinduism. The superstructure of Hinduism is built upon the foundation of the Upanishads, the essence of the Vedic wisdom.

In the age of the Upanishads, *moksha* (liberation of the *atman*, or 'inner self', from physical limitations) became the ultimate goal of human life and the transcendent knowledge became the means. The knowledge of the inner self, the *atman*, was declared as the supreme knowledge. The Vedic deities and the Vedic sacrifices took the back seat and meditation, and contemplation on the cosmic absolute gained prominence. In this new spiritualized religion, *moksha* replaced heaven, higher knowledge superseded sacrifices, and the cosmic absolute represented the unity of all deities. The Law of Karma became the fundamental tenet of Hinduism.

The Sutra Period (1500 – 500 BCE)

The Upanishads were composed during this period and the basic texts (*Mimamsa, Nyaya, Sankhya* and *Brahma Sutra*), which later led to development of the six popular systems of Hindu philosophy, were developed during this period. The development of Buddhism and Jainism as a rebellion against the Vedic sacrifices and the powerful priesthood also took place around this time. Notably Buddha did not reject the Upanishads. He only rejected the Vedic sacrifices and authority of the priests. He never broke away entirely from Hinduism. He was born a Hindu, lived and died as a Hindu.

The Epic Period (600 BCE – 300 CE)

This period saw the development of the two great epics (the Ramayana and the Mahabharata with the spiritual masterpiece of the Bhagavad Gita), the Laws of Manu (social code), some minor Upanishads and some of the earliest Puranas (Hindu mythology). Through ancient stories and legends of the people, the epics brought the Upanishadic religion to the common people in concrete form that they could understand. The popular religion thus became theistic and was no longer predominantly sacrificial as in the *Brahmanas* or purely metaphysical as in the Upanishads. One of the most remarkable developments of this period was that all the gods and goddesses, worshipped by different people in various parts of the land, were incorporated into the Hindu pantheon as different manifestations of the supreme being. The three most important cosmic functions of the supreme being, creation, preservation and dissolution and recreation were associated with the three deities, Brahma, Vishnu, and Shiva, which gave rise to a Hindu Trinity.

Another remarkable development of this period was the doctrine of *avatars*, the belief that whenever the righteousness in the world declines, God takes the form of a human being to restore righteousness (see BG 4,7). The philosophy of theism was further strengthened through temple worship, pilgrimages to sacred places and celebration of festivals. Thus, temples replaced the sacrificial altars of the Vedic sacrifices and Brahmanism evolved into contemporary Hinduism.

The Age of the *Puranas* (300 – 500 CE)

The method of teaching religion through stories and legends became more popular and a host of Puranas (Hindu mythology) was composed during this period. Through incredible real-life stories and fantastic legends, Puranas brought the ideals of the Vedas and the Upanishads to the minds of the common people. Thus the abstract became concrete and imagination turned into devotion. Puranas contributed greatly to the process of popularization and systemization of Hindu religious thought. They became an excellent tool of instruction and entertainment, especially when their stories were read at large public gatherings and plays based on their stories enacted during festivals. Even today, the Puranas are read in homes and temples to provide religious instruction to the common people. For this reason, the Puranas are called the heart of popular Hinduism.

Another major development of this period was popularization of worship of the divine as the Mother Goddess. A unique class of literature, called Tantras, was developed, which became the scriptures of Shaktas, worshippers of the Divine Mother, one of the traditions of the contemporary Hinduism. Shaktism (worship of the Mother Goddess) represents synthesis of the pre-Vedic and Vedic elements of Hinduism. In contemporary Hinduism, diverse forms of the Divine Mother are worshipped as knowledge, wisdom, strength, love and compassion.

While the popular religion developed in accordance with the Puranas and the Tantras, together with their elaborate rites and rituals, the religion of the learned systemized the philosophical *Sutras* of the six popular schools of Hindu philosophy (Nyaya, Vaisheshika, Sankhya, Yoga, Mimamsa and Vedanta). Each of these schools represents a unique view of life, and is called Darshana. The above Sutras together with their classical commentaries, which were composed later by their followers, gave rise to various comprehensive schools of Hindu philosophy.

Buddhism dies in India (750 – 1000 CE)

During this period, Buddhism finally died in India, the land of its own birth. One of the major reasons for its demise was that it took away the deity, object of worship, which could satisfy the longing of the human heart, from the people. Buddhism's overemphasis on monastic life and the substitution of individual reason as a guide in religious matters over for the authority of the Vedas did not help it either.

Two strong devotional movements rose in South India during this period and significantly strengthened the theistic thought of Hinduism. One was led by the twelve mystic poets, called Alvars, the followers of Vaishnavaism, and the other by 63 (a traditional number) mystic poets called Nayanars, the followers of Shaivism. With the joy of their religious experiences, intense devotion to God and utter humility, these mystic poets wandered from town to town in South India, singing the hymns of their fiery devotion to God. These wandering singers slowly and surely cut the roots of the atheistic creeds of Buddhism and Jainism in India.

While Alvars and Nayanars drove away Buddhism in India on the grounds of devotion to God, Adi Shankaracharya (or Shankara) defeated Buddhism on the grounds of philosophy. Shankaracharya was born in South India in about 788 CE. He renounced the world at an early age, became a religious teacher and established the Advaita Vedanta (strict monism) school of philosophy, which is based on the Upanishads, Vedanta Sutra (aphorisms on the Upanishads) and the Bhagavad Gita. He travelled all over India expounding Advaita Vedanta, which is a masterpiece of spiritual insight and intellectual subtlety. He established four monasteries, which are to this day the popular centres of religious education and philosophical research in India. Besides being one of the greatest philosophers the world has ever seen, Shankara was also a religious reformer, an ardent devotee, who composed hymns of passionate devotion to the deities he worshipped, and a champion of orthodox Vedic faith. He opposed soulless rituals, godless Buddhism and repulsive forms of many other traditions which existed in his time. He brought Bhagavad Gita to the forefront and popularized it among ordinary people.

Devotional Movement (1000 – 1800 CE)

This period is marked by a strong devotional movement that swept entire India, first in the southern and later in the northern part of the country. The passionate devotional hymns of Alvars inspired Ramanujacharya, a popular saint and philosopher of southern India, to establish a system of philosophy, which is called Vishishtadvaita (qualified monism). Unlike Shankara, who gave more importance to knowledge, Ramanujacharya emphasized love of God and absolute self-surrender as quickest way to enlightenment. The devotion-based theistic philosophy of Ramanujacharya attracted many followers including the lower classes of the society of his day, who adopted Vaishnavaism in large numbers. Not satisfied by the strict monism of Shankara or the qualified-monism of Ramanujacharya, a strictly dualistic (Dvaita) philosophy was established by Madhavacharya, another popular saint and religious reformer of southern India.

The devotional movement in the northern part of India centred around two incarnations, Rama and Krishna, of Lord Vishnu. Ramananda, a popular saint, was the leader of the movement that centres on devotion to Rama. He taught that enlightenment could be gained by repeating the sacred name of Rama. He inspired two great men of his time, Kabir (a Muslim mystic) and Guru Nanak, a popular saint, who later founded Sikhism. Ramananda also established an order of ascetics, called Ramanandis, to which belonged Tulsi Das, the celebrated author of the famous Hindi version of Ramayana.

The devotion that centres on Krishna was made popular by a large number of mystic poets and saints, such as Chandidas, Mira Bai, Vallabha and Chaitanya. The devotional movement continued to advance for a long time, producing numerous saints, sects and devotional poetry in many Indian languages.

Contemporary Hinduism

Contemporary Hinduism is not only the religion of the Vedas, but also of the epics, Puranas, and teachings of ancient, medieval and the modern sages and saints. Although numerous experiences and expressions of various periods have been synthesized into modern Hinduism, the broad definition of contemporary Hinduism is nearly the same as it was in the Vedic period. The belief in *karma, dharma, samsara*, reverence for sacred scriptures, acceptance of the religious obligation to satisfy one's ancestors with progeny, acceptance of other faiths as valid paths for enlightenment, and adhering to *dharma* to attain spiritual perfection (*moksha*) are essentially the same as they were in the Vedic period. The major change from the Vedic mode of life is that the focus on sacrifices in the Vedic period has now shifted to the worship and devotional expression to a popular set of Hindu deities such as Shiva, Vishnu, Rama, Krishna and the Mother Goddess in many forms such as Lakshmi, Saraswati, Durga and Kali. One of the notable features of Hinduism is that it utilizes guidance of its sages and saints to adapt to the environment without affecting its core values. The focus of Hinduism has always been spiritual experience and not religious authority. In this sense, Hinduism is not a tradition of persons, but of principles.

History has not been so kind to Hindus and Hinduism in India. First came Muslim invaders in the early eleventh century, who conquered and ruled the country for six centuries. They brought their crusading religion, forcibly converted Hindus to Islam, demolished Hindu temples and destroyed holy places. Tens of thousands of Hindus who refused to be converted were put to the sword. The Muslim occupation was the greatest disaster that overtook Hinduism in the course of its history. The Hindu society became paralysed and many social evils crept in. Then came the British rule, which lasted for a century and a half. British rule created a different sort of problem altogether. Firstly, they robbed India of its riches and left the country bankrupt before granting it independence. Secondly, the Christian missionaries, backed by enormous economic and political power, tried to convert Hindus to Christianity. To help their occupation, the British wanted to create a new breed of Indians who would be Indian in blood and colour, but English in thought, action, taste and temperament. Hindus, especially the younger generation, began imitating the English way of life. During these dark days of Hindu history the religion became stagnant, fettered with customs and restrictions, which were looked upon as the Laws of God. This situation was eventually corrected by diligent efforts of a host of heroes of the Hindu renaissance.

The morning star of the modern Hindu renaissance was Ram Mohan Roy (1772–1833), often called the father of modern India. He brought about the abolition of the cruel social custom of *sati* (burning widows on the funeral pyre of their husbands, which had no sanction in any religious text), emphasized the value of modern scientific education, and denounced soulless rituals, idol worship and the caste system. He founded Brahmo Samaj, a school of rational theism, embodying the Upanishadic vision of Hinduism. Roy's successor was Debendranath Tagore (called Maharshi), father of the Noble Prize laureate Rabindranath Tagore. Maharshi valued the Upanishads, but broke with the orthodox tradition by declaring that the Veda was not infallible. Later under the leadership of Keshub Chander Sen (1838–84), Brahmo Samaj became more Christian than Hindu and many members left in protest, with the result that the organization split into various groups and lost its influence in India.

Swami Dayananda Sarasvati (1824–83) introduced a dynamic type of Hinduism based upon the Vedas to spread Vedic culture. He denounced idol worship, the caste system, and marriage of young brides to much older grooms. He declared that only the Vedas teach the truth and laid down the principles of Sanatana Dharma (the original name of Hinduism) based upon teachings of the Vedas, Upanishads, Manusmriti and some Dharmashastras, but excluded the epics and Puranas. He founded the Arya Samaj movement in 1875 and launched an aggressive movement to reconvert Hindus who had been converted by Muslim and Christian missionaries. He performed *shuddhi* ceremonies (purification rites) on thousands of converts to bring them back to Hinduism.

Annie Besant (1847–1933) played an important role in modern Hindu renaissance. Through her numerous talks and writings, she brought out the true teachings of Hinduism to the forefront at a time when Hinduism was being attacked from all sides. She translated and popularized the Bhagavad Gita and started a Hindu college in Benares, which later expanded to what is now Benares Hindu University, a prestigious institution of both religious and secular education in India.

Sri Ramakrishna (1836–86), one of the eminent sages of India and recognized by many Hindus as an *avatar* (incarnation of God), was a mystical devotee of Kali (the Divine Mother). He uplifted Hinduism by his marvellous discourses which are recorded in the *Gospel of Sri Ramakrishna*, a spectacular resource on Hindu religious tradition. He spoke with authority based on his own religious experience. He experimented with various spiritual paths, including those of Islam and Christianity, and attained the same results. Thus he became a living synthesis of all religions and taught true Sanatana Dharma which sees historical religions as only different aspects. Ramakrishna was not a scholar and had not received any formal education. All his knowledge came from oral tradition and his own spiritual experience. He initiated his leading disciple Swami Vivekananda to continue the mission of revival and regeneration of Hinduism.

Swami Vivekananda (1863–1902) was a great saint, scholar, religious reformer and the favourite disciple of Sri Ramakrishna. Vivekananda had great successes at the World Parliament of Religions held in Chicago in 1893, where he introduced the universal message of Hinduism to the West for the first time. Following his well-received talks at the Parliament, he toured America and Europe and on his return to India founded the Ramakrishna Mission to disseminate Hinduism's universal teachings. He applied his master's teachings to the problems of national life and established the Hindu order of *sannyasi* (renunciants) to set an example for not only religious practice, but also for social service and relief work. He worked tirelessly both inside and outside India to illustrate the essential doctrines of Hinduism. Today the Ramakrishna mission is a well-organized and well-respected institution worldwide, maintaining colleges, schools, hospitals and publishing enormous amount of religious and spiritual literature for the seekers of truth. It has over one hundred centres in many parts of the world.

Sri Aurobindo Ghose (1872–1950), also called Maharishi, was a freedom-fighter-turned sage, who reinterpreted the Hindu concepts of moksha, yoga, and *jivanmukti* (a state of an individual who has attained moksha while still in its human body) in the light of his own spiritual experience. He taught that human minds must be raised to higher consciousness (which he called Life Divine) in order to solve political, social and economic problems which plague human society today. Ordinary human consciousness is not capable of solving these global problems permanently, Aurobindo wrote. Like the *rishis* (seers) of the ancient times, he gave up his active work, settled down in Pondicherry in South India and built an ashram (hermitage), then for forty years taught Integral Yoga for the transformation of human consciousness. People came from many parts of the world to seek his help. Later Aurobindo's followers developed the city of Auroville in South India to put his spiritual principles into practice.

Rabindranath Tagore (1861–1941), awarded the Noble Prize for literature, was one of the greatest mystic poets of the world. His inspiration came from the Upanishads, the Bhagavad Gita and devotional songs of the Vaishnava poets of Bengal. The universal vision of the Upanishads is reflected in his poetry. His discourses in *Sadhana* are a modern commentary on the Upanishads. In his later life he travelled all over the world denouncing aggressive nationalism as a crime against humanity.

Mahatma Gandhi (1861–1948) was not only an architect of India's freedom and the prophet of non-violence, as the world generally knows him. He was also a great religious reformer. He taught love of God, service to community and the practice of *ahimsa* (non-violence). *Ahimsa* had always been a cardinal virtue of Hinduism but previously had only been applied to individual action. Gandhi extended *ahimsa* to communities and nations. 'The path of non-violence requires much more courage than violence,' Gandhi wrote (Prabhu and Rao 1997). He taught that truth is god and god is truth, and non-violence is the path to reach it.

Ramana Maharshi (1879–1950), another Hindu spiritual genius and a well-known teacher of Advaita Vedanta, has had a profound spiritual impact on the West. He was not educated in the traditional sense. His deep spiritual influence was charged with the power of his own spiritual experience. Maharishi was first introduced to the West through the writings of Paul Brunton, a British journalist, who authored many works including *Maharishi and His Message* and *Passage to India*.

Sarvepalli Radhakrishnan (1888–1975), a former President of India and a well-known writer and scholar of both Eastern and Western philosophies, presented purified, spiritualized and non-sectarian Hinduism through his numerous speeches and writings. Talking about true religion he wrote, 'The half-religious and irreligious fight about dogmas and not truly religious. The more religious we grow, the more tolerant of diversity shall we become.' (Radhakrishnan 1926)

Bhaktivinode Thakur (1838–1914) was a prominent magistrate under British rule in India. After studying the life of Chaitanya (a sixteenth century saint revered in India), which ignited the flame of love of God (in the form of Radha and Krishna) in his heart, he dedicated his life with tenacity to re-establishing Vaisnava practices in West Bengal and Orissa in India. He wrote many Vaishnava texts, songs and poems. At the end of the nineteenth century, he envisaged a time when Indian and Western devotees would dance together chanting the holy names of Krishna.

A.C. Bhaktivedanta Swami (1896–1977) was born in West Bengal, India. As a grand-disciple of Bhaktivinode Thakur, he patiently prepared throughout his life to bring Vaishnavism to the West. He was a prolific writer and translated many original Vaishnava texts, including Bhagavad Gita, Srimad Bhagavatam and Chaitanya Caritamrita, into English. He travelled to New York as an elderly monk and yet inspired the youth of the 1960s to adopt a life of spiritual principles. The International Society for Krishna Consciousness was founded in 1965 and from small beginnings the Hare Krishna movement spread world wide igniting interest in Vedic practices and philosophy. Numerous temples have been established across the world and his books have been translated into seventy different languages making ancient Vedic Vaisnava tradition available to all.

All the different traditions of Hinduism discussed above coexist in contemporary Hinduism like the branches of a tree. The trunk of the tree of Hinduism is made of its core doctrines such as dharma, karma, belief in the divinity of soul, and unity of existence. Hinduism is essentially a democratic tradition and it allows each group to attain truth through its own faith by means of discipline of the mind and morals. Despite all the changes Hinduism has undergone throughout the ages, it has always nourished its unifying principle, which allows it to be faithful to itself while sharing whatever treasures the other faiths may possess.

Chapter 2

Hindu Scriptures

> Whenever I have read any part of the Vedas, I have felt
> that some unearthly and unknown light illuminated me.
> In the great teachings of the Vedas, there is no touch of
> sectarianism. It is of all ages, climes, and nationalities
> and is the royal road for attainment of the Great
> Knowledge. When I am at it, I feel that I am under the
> spangled heavens of a summer night.
>
> Henry David Thoreau (1817–62)

Unlike other religions of the world, Hinduism has many scriptures. This is because Hinduism was not founded by one prophet or incarnation of God. Hindu scriptures, the most ancient writings in the world, are of two categories: Sruti (primary scriptures) and Smriti (secondary scriptures). Sruti (meaning 'that which is heard') are of divine origin (sacred revelations) and 'were heard' by ancient rishis (sages) in their deep meditations. Sruti are the governing source of Hindu religious beliefs and practices and include the Vedas, Upanishads (concluding portions of the Vedas) and the Bhagavad Gita, which is the essence of the Upanishads. Smriti (meaning 'that which is remembered') are of human origin and were written to explain the Sruti and make them understandable and meaningful to general population. All authoritative writings outside the Vedas are collectively referred to as Smriti, and include seven distinct groups of writings as shown in Figure 1.

Vedas

Veda is the source of Hindu tradition. 'To feel the pulse of Hinduism and to understand its subtleties, one must study the literature of the Vedas. In quality, in quantity, in significance for man's intellectual, cultural and spiritual life, this literature [Vedas] in its totality is unsurpassed among all other literary traditions of the world,' notes

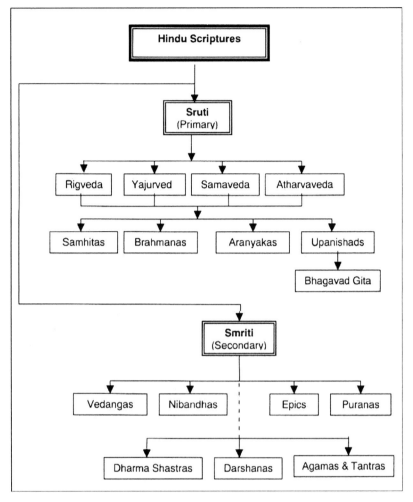

Figure 1.

Thomas Berry, a historian of Eastern spiritual traditions and culture. Veda means 'knowledge' and the Vedas include supreme knowledge of Hinduism in the form of hymns and chants containing religious and spiritual insights of ancient sages and seers. Vedas are the 'revelation' and command unquestionable authority in Hinduism. To derive mystic power and full spiritual benefit from the Vedas, the Vedic hymns must be recited with exact wording, with correctly prescribed pitch, and with correct sounds and syllables. In order to provide proper training for recitation of the Vedas, auxiliary sciences, the Vedangas, were developed as a part of the training for Vedic priests. There are four Vedas: Rigveda, Yajurveda, Samaveda, and Atharvaveda. Each Veda consists of four parts: Samhitas (or Mantras), Brahmanas, Aranyakas, and Upanishads.

The Samhitas are made up of hymns and utterances called Mantras, which were revealed to ancient rishis (Vedic seers) and are the expression of what has been experienced through intuitive perception. The Brahmanas are elaborations of the earlier Vedic writings. They emphasize and discuss the rituals and correct techniques for their performance, and reveal the mystic power of the Vedic rites, rituals and sacraments. The Aranyakas provide mystical interpretations of the Mantras and rituals and were put together in the seclusion of the forest ashramas. For this reason, Aranyakas are also called 'the forest books.' The Upanishads are the concluding portions of the Vedas and include supreme knowledge of self-realization.

Rigveda

Rigveda, meaning the 'Veda of Adoration', is the first of the four Vedas and is humanity's oldest surviving religious record. It comprises ten books, containing 10,417 verses, arranged as 1017 hymns in 20 groups. Rigveda contains hymns of joyous wonder at the manifestations of Nature and adorations of the Vedic deities, with two-thirds of the hymns addressed to Agni (deity of fire) and Indra (ruler of the Vedic deities). Other deities include Rudra, the two Ashvins, Surya, Varuna, the Maruts and the Ribhus. A Vedic deity is a personification of the infinite power and wisdom of the creator as a dynamic force in Nature.

The hymns of the Rigveda were revealed to the rishis (Vedic seers) of yore. The most prominent of these rishis are Viswamitra, Vasishta, and Bhardwaj. Since these rishis did not write the hymns down, the Vedas were transmitted from one generation to another by word of mouth for thousands of years until Rishi Vyasa finally collected all the hymns and arranged them in the order that they exist today. Even today there are special Vedic priests in India, known as *strotriyas*, who learn the Vedas by heart. 'If every manuscript of the Rigveda were lost, we should be able to recover the whole of it from the memory of the *strotriyas* in India. These native students learn the Veda by heart and they learn it from the mouth of their guru, and never from the written manuscript,' writes Max Müller in his book *India, what can it teach us?* (Müller 2000).

The Rigveda shows that the Vedic seers approached their deities not only as friends, as servants to their masters, as sons and daughters to their fathers and mothers, but also as the lover to the beloved. Rigveda reflects a sense of intimate communion between the Vedic visionaries and Nature. The following is one of the most popular hymns of the Rigveda, which provides the basis for Hinduism's reverence for other religions of the world as being different paths to the same Reality (RV 1.164,46):

> They call Him as Indra, as Mitra, as Varuna, as Agni,
> and as that divine and noble-winged Garutman. Truth is
> one, the wise call it by various names, whether as Agni,
> or as Yama, or as Matarisvan.

(Note: Indra, Mitra, Varuna, Agni, Garutman, Yama, and Matarisvan are names of the Vedic deities)

Yajurveda

Yajurveda deals with Vedic worship (*yajna*) and includes acts of worship such as oblations made to Agni (deity of fire). It provides instructions for correct performance of rituals and is thus an important text for Hindu priests. While hymns of the Yajurveda are mostly from the Rigveda, there is a significant variation in their content and arrangement.

Yajurveda includes two branches, Krishna Yajurveda and Shukla Yajurveda. The literary value of Yajurveda is mostly in its prose, which consists of short sentences of profound meaning and rhythm. The Krishna Yajurveda is divided into seven books (*kandas*) of forty-four chapters. The Shukla Yajurveda consists of forty chapters. The following is one of the popular hymns of the Yajurveda, which Hindus use in the sacred fire ceremony for the good of all people. This hymn invokes the universal presence of the supreme being and was used by Nobel laureate Rabinderanath Tagore to set the following motto for his university in India: 'Into it the whole universe comes as into a single nest.'

> That [the primal Cause of the Universe] is itself Fire and
> Sun; That itself is the Wind and Moon; That itself is the
> Veda and Knowledge; those waters and Creator are
> That. For Him, there is no counterpart [or image]; great
> indeed is His glory. The wise man sees that eternal thing
> in the recesses of his heart; into it the whole universe

comes as into a single nest; there, all this universe is gathered [at dissolution] and is thrown out [at creation; 'Big Bang'?]; that all-pervading Being is woven into beings as the warp and the woof.

Yajurveda XXXII.1–12

Samaveda

Samaveda consists of a selection of poetry mainly from the Rigveda with some text of its own. It contains verses addressed to the three Vedic deities Agni (fire), Indra (king of gods) and Soma (energizing herb). The verses are divided in two parts, Purva-Archika (first adoration) and Uttar-Archika (later adoration) and are to be recited by specifically indicated melodies using the seven notes (*svaras*). Samaveda is the oldest form of Indian music and the source of the later traditions of Indian music. Hindus believe that music is an aid in the practice of meditation and attainment of enlightenment.

Atharvaveda

Atharvaveda, meaning the 'Veda of the Wise and the Old,' is associated with the name of an ancient 'Wise and the Old' sage-poet, Atharvan. This Veda is also called Atharva-Angirasa, being associated with the name of another rishi, Angirasa. This Veda contains about six thousand verses forming 731 poems with a small portion in prose. About one-seventh of the Atharvaveda text is common to the Rigveda.

Atharvaveda glorifies the curative powers of herbs and waters in poetic hymns composed by the visionary sage-poets of the ancient times. These poems constitute the first poetry of the human race. Many poems relate to human diseases and to natural herbs and magic amulets, which remove such diseases. There are poems relating to atonement of sins, expiation for errors and omissions committed in performing rites and rituals, and for mistakes and miscalculations committed in politics and other fields of human interest. Atharvaveda contains hymns for securing success in agriculture, trade and other human activities, and for creating love and understanding in human relations. Among numerous wonderful hymns of Atharvaveda, the following is a peace hymn often recited by Hindus for the good of humanity:

Peaceful be the Earth, peaceful be air, peaceful be heaven, peaceful be the waters and peaceful be the trees. May all gods bring peace! May there be peace through these invocations of peace. With these invocations of peace, which pacify everything, I render peaceful whatever here is terrible, whatever here is cruel, and whatever here is sinful. Let it become auspicious, and let everything be beneficial to us.

Atharvaveda XIX.9

Upanishads

The Upanishads are humanity's most profound philosophical inquiry and are also called Vedanta, meaning 'end of the Vedas.' They are literally the end of the Vedas as they are the concluding portions. They are allegorically also the 'end of the Vedas', i.e. knowledge, since they are Hinduism's supreme spiritual truths. In the opinion of Hindus, there is no knowledge higher than the Upanishads.

Upanishad literally means, 'sitting near and receiving secret knowledge.' Upanishadic truths were transmitted by great seers of the past to their disciples, who sat near their gurus and received the highest knowledge directly from them. Vedic literature is divided into two divisions, Karmakanda and Jnanakanda. The former deals with karma (human action) and includes *samhitas* (hymns) and *brahmanas* (commentaries); the latter deals with *jnana* (knowledge) in the form of the Aranyakas and the Upanishads. Thus each Upanishad is associated with a Veda, such as Isa Upanishad with Shukla Yajurveda, and Kena Upanishad with Samaveda.

Nobody knows with certainty how many Upanishads originally existed. A total of 108 have been preserved of which the following ten are considered principal Upanishads: Isa, Kena, Katha, Prasna, Mundaka, Mandukya, Taittiriya, Aitareya, Chandogya and Brhadaryanyaka. The teachings of the Upanishads together with those of the Bhagavad Gita, which itself is a summary of the Upanishads, form the basis of the Vedanta philosophy of Hinduism, which is not only popular in India, but also in the West. The Isa Upanishad emphasizes the identity of the human soul with the divine soul. The Kena Upanishad discusses qualities of the divine essence (*brahman*) and its relationship with gods and goddesses. The Katha Upanishad, through the famous story of Nachiketa, discusses death and the permanence of the soul (atman). The fairly long Chandogya Upanishad develops the doctrine of transmigration of the soul. The

Brhadaryanyaka Upanishad, the longest of the Upanishads, concludes that the physical phenomenon is the product of pure consciousness as the ultimate source and fullness of the source is not affected by emergence of the phenomenon.

Bhagavad Gita

The Bhagavad Gita, the sacred scripture that is often called the Bible of the Hindus, is one of the three pillars of Hinduism (with the Upanishads and the Brahma Sutras as the other two). The Bhagavad Gita is a spiritual dialogue between Sri Krishna, a Hindu incarnation of God, and Arjuna, one of the heroes of the Mahabharata, an ancient Hindu epic. An anonymous Hindu saint has described the Bhagavad Gita in the following words: 'If the Upanishads are the cows, the Lord Himself the milker, Arjuna the calf, those of purified understanding are the drinkers of the milk, the supreme nectar of the Gita.' Since the Bhagavad Gita represents a summary of the Upanishadic teachings, it is sometimes called an Upanishad of the Upanishads.

The two words Bhagavad and Gita mean 'the song of the Lord.' The Bhagavad Gita, however, is not a lyric, but a spiritual poem. This scripture is a part of the Hindu epic Mahabharata, composed by Sage Vyasa in about 300 BCE. However, the great Mahabharata war took place much earlier, around 3067 BCE. The Bhagavad Gita has inspired countless Hindus since its composition. It has also inspired many Western thinkers, such as Henry David Thoreau (1817–62), Ralph Waldo Emerson (1803–82), and Maxine Elliott (1871–1940). Although the original date of composition of the Bhagavad Gita is not clear, its teachings are timeless, and as such, the exact time of the revelation of this scripture is of little spiritual significance. The original text of the Bhagavad Gita is in Sanskrit, but translations are available in all major languages of the world. The first English translation was performed by Charles Wilkins in 1785.

The setting of the Bhagavad Gita is the battlefield of Kurukshetra, about one hundred miles north-west of modern day Delhi in India. It consists of 700 Sanskrit *slokas* (verses) arranged in eighteen chapters. It is a book of *jnana*, *bhakti*, and karma (light, love, and life). If a person were to be given an instruction manual telling him how to live life on Earth, the Gita would indeed be such a manual: 'Who are we? Why are we born? What is the goal of life? What are the means? What are good and bad actions? What should we do when one duty conflicts with another?' These and many other questions are raised and answered in the Bhagavad Gita. The Bhagavad Gita is a spiritual classic as Wilhelm von Humboldt puts it, 'The most beautiful, perhaps the only true philosophical song existing in any known tongue, perhaps the deepest and loftiest thing the world has to show.'

Vedangas, Dharma Shastras and Nibandhas

Vedangas, meaning 'the limbs of the Vedas', are auxiliary texts and include subjects such as correct pronunciation, metre, etymology, grammar, astronomy, and rules for rites and rituals. Dharma Shastras describe the codes of human conduct, righteousness, personal hygiene, social administration, ethics and moral duties. The best-known writing of this category is Manu Smriti, the Laws of Manu. Nibandhas are the digests, manuals and encyclopaedias of the Vedic laws pertaining to human conduct, worship and rituals. They also include topics such as gift giving, pilgrimages, and the maintenance of the human body.

Puranas

Purana means 'ancient.' There are 18 major Puranas: Brahma, Padma, Vishnu, Bhagavata, Narda, Markandeya, Agni, Bhavishya, Brahmavaivarta, Linga, Varaha, Skanda, Vamna, Kurma, Matsya, Garuda, Brahmanda, and Vayu. They were written over a long period of time and constitute Hindu mythology. One of the most popular Puranas, that has made a profound impression on the minds of Hindus to this day, is the Bhagavata Purana, which is associated with the life of Sri Krishna, a Hindu incarnation of God. Bhagavata Purana has given rise to innumerable songs of devotion, dramas and dances all connected with the childhood and youth of Krishna. It is said that if the Bhagavad Gita is for the intellectuals, Bhagavata Purana is for the ordinary people.

Although Puranas are called secondary scriptures, they are not scriptures in the narrow sense scriptures are understood in other religions. They were written in ancient times to expound teachings of the primary scriptures (Sruti) for the benefit of those, who could not comprehend deep philosophy of the primary scriptures. Some of the Puranas are based upon true-life stories of the ancient kings, queens, and heroes. Others are based upon imagery and imagination. In Puranas, neither genuineness of the character is important, nor purity and truthfulness of the story. Only the moral is important. This is why there are some popular Puranic stories, where even gods are depicted as unkind, power-hungry and revengeful, and in some cases outright mean and partial. However, when we look at the morals of the Puranic stories, they are inspiring, meaningful and wonderful. Whether a Puranic story is true or not is immaterial for Hindus. The following is an example of an incredible Puranic story that brings forth profound spiritual truths.

Story

Once Ganesha (elephant-headed Hindu deity – see Chapter 3) ate too many *modakas* (sweets) offered to him by his devotees and his belly inflated and bulged. He rode his mouse (Ganesha's vehicle) and proceeded home. Suddenly the mouse saw a snake crossing the road in front of him. Terrified, the mouse jumped backward causing Ganesha to fall down. Ganesha's large belly hit the ground and split open, thus scattering his *modakas* on the ground in all directions. Ganesha was enraged and he killed the snake, collected the *modakas*, and tied his split belly with the snake's body. The moon, which had been watching this scene all this time, laughed out loudly, which enraged Ganesha further. He pulled out one of his tusks and threw it at the moon, causing darkness all over the Earth. The gods, who became distressed with darkness, appealed to Ganesha to take back his tusk and restore the moon. Ganesha agreed on the condition that the moon gain and lose its light by waxing and waning each month to suffer the punishment. The interpretation of the myth in Hindu spiritual lore is as follows.

Interpretation

An ego-driven mind believes that peace and happiness in this world can be attained by amassing material wealth (symbolized by Ganesha's belly overfilled with *modakas*). The ego rejoices in the worldly possessions (symbolized by Ganesha riding the mouse and proceeding home happily), but develops fear (symbolized by the mouse seeing the snake walking in front of him) that if his wealth were lost, he would become poor and miserable. The mouse jumps backwards at the sight of the snake and knocks Ganesha down. This conveys the idea that when ego is attacked by fear, the man plunges into despair.

Ganesha's falling on the ground and his belly splitting symbolizes the devastation that is caused by fear. The higher self is always watching what is happening to the individual (symbolized by the moon's loudly laughing at Ganesha) and provides necessary help (grace) to restore the man. When the man comes to senses with the help of divine grace, he throws away the fear (symbolized by Ganesha's killing the snake and tying the snake's body around his torn belly) and gathers his thoughts, i.e. restores the mind (symbolized by Ganesha gathering the scattered *modakas*).

Ganesha has two tusks, the right tusk symbolizes reason and the left tusk symbolizes emotion. Ganesha throws his left tusk at the moon (symbolizing the surrender of ego by an individual), which produces immediate mental and nervous relaxation (symbolized by darkness that resulted when Ganesha threw his tusk at moon.) Ganesha did not throw the right tusk (reason), i.e. he did not surrender reason, only emotion. Hindu spiritual tradition maintains that reason is an important tool for one's spiritual pursuit. Ganesha's taking the tusk back and restoring the moon conveys the idea that when ego is surrendered, one gets immediate peace and relaxation (symbolized by darkness that Earth is submerged in). With the surrender of the ego dawns the wisdom, and one realizes that moderation is the best philosophy of life on Earth. This is taught by Sri Krishna in the Bhagavad Gita: 'Arjuna, this yoga is neither for him who overeats, nor for him who observes a complete fast; it is neither for him who is given to too much sleep, nor even for him who is ceaselessly awake.' In the above legend, the waxing and waning of the moon symbolizes the life of moderation in this world of duality.

Epics

The two great epics of Hinduism are the Ramayana and the Mahabharata. These are the most important scriptures of popular Hinduism. Ramayana deals with the life story of Sri Rama, one of the most revered incarnations of Lord Vishnu (the ultimate reality). Ramayana was originally written by sage Valmiki, who is also known as Adi Kavi (the first poet).

Mahabharata is a massive literary work attributed to the ancient sage Vedavyasa. The tradition says that Vedavyasa dictated Mahabharata to Ganesha, who wrote it down for the masses. Mahabharata is a story of the great ancient war that took place between the Kauravas and the Pandavas around 3,000 BCE in India.

Darshanas

These are the writings of the six popular schools of Hindu philosophy: Uttara Mimamsa, Purva Mimamsa, Sankhya, Yoga, Nyaya, and Vaisheshika. These writings codify, interpret and provide logical arguments to support different spiritual experiences of ancient seers as recorded in the Vedas. Each Darshana possesses a highly technical terminology and is attributed to its founder, including a number of commentaries written later by the followers of these schools.

Sectarian scriptures

The sectarian scriptures chiefly include the scriptures of the three main *sampradayas* (sects) of Shaivism, Vaishnavism, and Shaktism and are called Agamas or Tantras. Each of these scriptures generally has four parts and deals with religious and philosophical beliefs, meditative practices, and construction of temples and installation of deities.

Chapter 3

The Hindu View of the Ultimate Reality

> Is there a God? This is as foolish as one asking, 'Have I a father?' The very fact that you exist is enough proof that you must have had a father.
>
> Swami Chinmayananda (Chinmayananda 2000: 149)

What is the ultimate reality? This has different answers given by different religions. These answers include a wide spectrum of concepts such as mysterious forces of nature, a supreme ruler who must be feared and worshipped, a loving father who sent his only son to spread his message, a formless creator, the beneficent and merciful, and the unborn, uncreated, eternal being, who can be experienced only through silence. Hindus maintain that all these descriptions of the ultimate reality are correct, but incomplete. Describing the ultimate reality in words is like trying to compress an ocean into a test tube. It just cannot be done. In the language of mythology, if Saraswati (Hindu deity of knowledge) were to use the waters of all the oceans as ink, all trees of the planet Earth as pens, and the entire space of the cosmos as paper, she would be unable to provide a complete description of the ultimate reality.

If we analyze the different answers given by different religions, we are led to the view that the divine is either the impersonal reality (absolute) or the personal reality (God). The spiritual experiences of the majority of the sages and seers of all religions and cultures generally favour the former viewpoint, whereas the ethical theism favours the latter. With regard to the nature of the ultimate reality, the Upanishad says, 'There the sight does not travel, nor speech, nor mind. It is unknown and inexplicable. The absolute is beyond known and unknown. Thus we have heard from the wise who taught us That.' (Ken-U 1,3) The human mind, which is logical and rational, is not willing to accept the idea that the absolute is totally incomprehensible. Hindu religious thought emphasizes the transcendent nature of the absolute but rejects the idea that the absolute is remote to the world and thus altogether transcendent. What then is our relationship with the divine?

A human being uses his mind to bring down the unknown to the realm of the known. To him, the human is an imperfect personality (*pursha*), whereas the absolute is the perfect personality (*uttama pursha*). Since human personality consists of cognition, emotion, and will, there is a logical necessity to conceive a personal God, who is the supreme knower, supreme lover, and possessor of the supreme will. In line with this thought, Hindu religious tradition affirms the personal aspect of the supreme being, but also reminds us of the impersonal or the supra-personal aspect of the divine (see Figure 2).

In the Hindu attitude towards the personal God, who is the adorable lord of the universe and who resides in the hearts of all beings, there is room for imagination of different kinds of personal relationships, such as that of the father and son or daughter, of friend and friend, of lovers, of husband and wife, and of master and servant. At the same time, there is a profound feeling in the heart of a Hindu that the lord and the devotee are essentially one in nature.

As early as the Rigveda, the Hindu mind has recognized that the eternally existent one supreme being has manifold attributes and manifestations. This idea is articulated in the Rigveda (RV 1.164, 46), which recognizes that the ultimate reality possesses infinite potential, power and intelligence and, as such, cannot be limited by a single name or form. Hindu scriptures refer to the impersonal aspect of ultimate reality as *nirguna brahman* (reality without attributes). Since this aspect of the ultimate reality has no attributes, it is not an object of prayer, but of meditation and knowledge. *Nirguna brahman* is the nameless and formless ultimate reality, and is beyond the human conception, beyond reasoning and beyond thought. *Nirguna brahman* is the infinite field of pure potentiality, the ultimate principle underlying the universe and is also called by other names such as the cosmic absolute, supreme being, universal spirit, and higher self.

Hindus call the personal aspect of ultimate reality *saguna brahman*, i.e. reality with attributes. *Saguna brahman* is the creator, sustainer and controller of the universe. Again, *saguna brahman* cannot be limited by one name or form and is, therefore, worshipped by various names and in various forms, both male and female. From the male aspect, *saguna brahman* is called by many Sanskrit names, such as *ishvara, parameshvara, paramatma, maheshvara, and purusha*. These Sanskrit

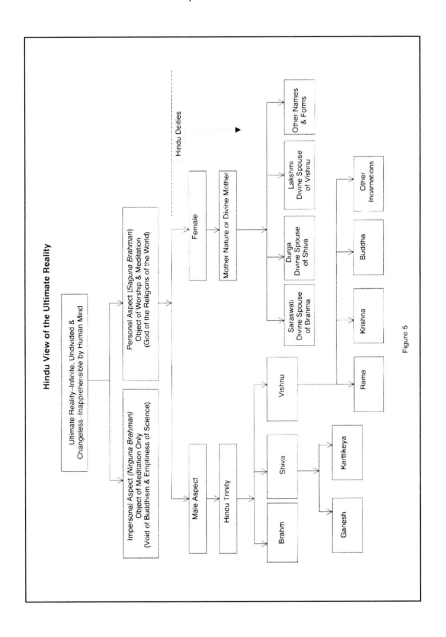

Figure 2.

names represent more or less the same concept as the word 'God' in other religions.

From the female standpoint, Hindus worship the personal aspect of the ultimate reality (hereafter in this chapter referred to as God) by various names, such as the Divine Mother, Durga and Kali. Hindus recognize both male and female aspects of God in various forms, called deities (or gods and goddesses – note small 'g'). A deity symbolizes one or more aspects of God. For example, Saraswati (see Figure 3) symbolizes the learning and knowledge aspect of God. Thus, if a Hindu wants to pray to God for knowledge and understanding, he prays to Saraswati for bestowing knowledge upon him. This does not mean that Saraswati (or any other Hindu deity) is separate from or independent of God. Just as sunlight cannot be conceived to have independent existence from the sun, a Hindu deity is not conceived to have a separate existence from God. Thus, Hindu deities symbolize various aspects of God and devotees have the freedom to worship whichever aspect of the divine they revere most, based upon their own mental constitution. There is only one God and he is the God of all. There is no other God. The Biblical statement 'Thou shalt have no other God before me,' really means, 'Thou shalt not convert life into something that is dead or suffer a known semblance of reality to be put in the place of reality,' explains Dr Radhakrishnan. (Radhakrishnan 1940: 337)

Hinduism is sometimes said to be the religion of 330 million gods. This misconception arises when people do not acquire a clear understanding of the symbolism of the Hindu pantheon. According to Hindu scriptures, the living beings are not apart from God, since God lives in each and every one of them in the form of the inner sprit (atman). Thus each living being is an individualized and particularized manifestation of God. In ancient times, it was believed that there were 330 million living beings. This gave rise to the concept of 330 million deities. Actually, 330 million deities could not have possibly been worshipped, since 330 million names could not have been constructed for them. The number 330 million was simply used to give a symbolic expression to the fundamental Hindu doctrine that God lives in the hearts of all living beings.

A Hindu uses a picture or an icon (usually made of metal, wood or clay) to symbolize a deity. The picture or the icon is used as an object of concentration to help the mind to concentrate on the worship, contemplation and meditation. The icon itself is not God, but serves as a symbol of God. 'We associate our ideas of infinity with the image of

Brahma

Rama   Krishna

Saraswati

Hanuman

Figure 3. Other Hindu deities.

Vishnu

Lakshmi

The syllable OM (or AUM) is the most sacred symbol of Hinduism. Both by its sound and form, it represents manifest and unmanifest *Brahman* and is therefore another name of *Atman* and *Brahman*.

'The Word [OM] is indeed Brahman. This Word is indeed the Supreme. He who knows this Word obtains whatever he desires.'

Katha Up 2, 16

OM or AUM

37

the blue sky, or of the sea. We also naturally connect our idea of holiness with the image of a church, a mosque, or a cross. The Hindus have associated the ideas of holiness, purity, truth, omnipresence with different images and forms,' explains Swami Vivekananda. (Vivekananda 1991) If somebody asks me, 'Where is the sky?' I would most probably raise my finger up pointing towards the sky. My finger is not the sky, but it points towards the sky. Similarly, an image or icon of God is not God, but a pointer, which directs the attention of the devotee towards the divine.

Hindu deity worship

Since ancient times Hindus have recognized that when the heart is absorbed in the love of God, the soul transcends the narrow bounds of religious dogma and is convinced of the infinite number of possible divine manifestations. This great truth led Hinduism to develop a universal outlook in its religious thought. As Dr Radhakrishnan explains, 'Hinduism is wholly free from the strange obsession of some faiths that the acceptance of a particular religious metaphysics is necessary for salvation, and non-acceptance thereof is a heinous sin meriting eternal punishment in hell.' (Radhakrishnan 1926: 28)

As the Hindu looks at various faiths in the world, he knows that the religious opinion of an individual depends on his inborn moral and intellectual capacity, training, education and environment. Thus Hinduism does not adopt force or threat to impose one way of worship, but uses suggestions and persuasion to teach religion and spirituality. When a Hindu approaches a guru (spiritual teacher) for guidance, the teacher suggests the student to choose a personal deity (*ishta devata*) that appeals to him or her the most. The teacher further advises the student that any divine name or form conceived symbolizes the absolute and sincere worship of the chosen deity gradually leads the worshipper to realize the absolute symbolized by the deity. The main purpose of Hindu deity worship is to develop one's spiritual consciousness and sensibility to truth.

The concept of worshipping God in the form of deities is unique to Hinduism. The Upanishads declare that God is infinite, undivided, and changeless. He is an absolute being beyond human description, although theologians may wish to put limits on him. Most people, however, cannot conceive the indescribable aspect of God and, therefore, cannot contemplate on him. The only tool we have for investigation of this higher truth is the mind, and the mind needs something in concrete form to think about and concentrate on. Hindu sages realized this difficulty early on and thus taught their disciples to worship God in whatever form they felt comfortable with. After all, the supreme lord who created this universe with all things and beings could also create a form for Himself to please His loving devotees.

In line with this thinking, Brahma was the name given to the supreme lord in Hindu scriptures for creating the universe, Vishnu for sustaining it and Shiva for dissolving it and recreating it all over again, in cycles. This led to worship of Brahma, Vishnu and Shiva as a Hindu Trinity. To help understand the concept of one God being called by various names, think of an everyday example. When you go to the office, you will probably wear smart clothes. When you work around the house, you are more likely to wear jeans and a T-shirt. If you play tennis, you may wear a short-sleeved shirt, shorts and tennis shoes. There are plenty more such examples. But the point here is that in all these cases you are the same person merely wearing different clothes to perform different tasks.

Similarly, the symbolic images of Brahma, Vishnu, Shiva and other Hindu deities are different forms of the supreme lord, the ultimate reality, conceived as performing various cosmic functions. The deities of other religions are only concerned with human destiny. The deities of Hinduism are symbols of cosmic energy and intelligence and are concerned not only with human destiny, but also with the destiny of all other beings of the world.

Traditional Hindu pantheon

The following are the traditional deities worshipped in Hinduism. This list is not all-inclusive, since many *sampradayas* (religious traditions) also use other names and forms for their worship.

Shiva, the first member of the Hindu Trinity, represents the aspect of the supreme being (the ultimate reality) that continuously dissolves to recreate in the cyclic process of creation, preservation, dissolution and recreation of the universe.

Vishnu, the second member of the Trinity, represents the cosmic power of the supreme being for preservation and sustenance of the universe.

Brahma, the third member of the Trinity, represents the creative power of the supreme being.

Sri Krishna: the eighth and the most popular incarnation of Vishnu.

Sri Rama: the seventh popular incarnation of Vishnu.

Durga: represents the power of the supreme being that preserves moral order and righteousness in creation.

Saraswati: goddess of knowledge and learning.

Lakshmi: goddess of material and spiritual wealth.

Sri Ganesha: represents the power of the supreme being that removes obstacles and ensures success in human endeavours.

Sri Hanuman: denotes the qualities of an ideal devotee of God.

Sri Subramanya Karttikeya: represents worldly prosperity as well as spiritual perfection

Symbolism of the Hindu pantheon

Just as a work of art reflects the imagination of the artist, the symbolism of the Hindu deities reflects the attributes and qualities of the ultimate reality as conceived by the ancient *rishis*. The symbolism of Hindu deities is subtle, sublime and profound; and when correctly understood, it greatly aids the devotee to realize the spiritual goal. The symbolism of Hindu deities can occupy a volume of its own. Because of the limited scope of this work, the symbolism of only the following three Hindu deities is illustrated below.

Sri Ganesha

Ganesha, the Hindu deity in a human form but with the head of an elephant, represents the power of the supreme being that removes obstacles and ensures success in human endeavours. For this reason, Hindus worship Ganesha first before beginning any religious, spiritual or worldly activity. In Hindu mythology, Ganesha is the first son of Shiva and Parvati, the Divine Mother. As explained below, the portrayal of Ganesha as the blend of human and animal parts symbolizes the ideals of perfection as conceived by Hindu sages and illustrates some philosophical concepts of profound spiritual significance.

Elephant head, wide mouth, and large ears

The large head of the elephant symbolizes wisdom, understanding, and a discriminating intellect that one must possess to attain perfection in life. The wide mouth represents natural human desire to enjoy life in the world. The large ears signify that a perfect person is the one who possesses a great capacity to listen to others and assimilate ideas.

The trunk and two tusks with the left tusk broken

There is no known human instrument that has an operating range as wide as that of an elephant's trunk. It can uproot a tree and yet lift a needle off the ground. Likewise, the human mind must be strong enough to face the ups and downs of the external world and yet delicate enough to explore the subtle realms of the inner world. The two tusks denote the two aspects of the human personality, wisdom and emotion. The right tusk represents wisdom and the left tusk represents emotion. The broken left tusk conveys the idea that one must conquer emotions with wisdom to attain perfection in life.

Elephant eyes

The elephant's eyes are said to possess natural deceptiveness that allows them to perceive objects to be bigger than what they really are. Thus the elephant's eyes symbolize the idea that even if an individual gets 'bigger and bigger' in wealth and wisdom, he should perceive others to be bigger than himself; that is, surrender one's pride and attain humility.

The four arms and various objects in the four hands

The four arms indicate that Ganesha is omnipresent and omnipotent. The left side of the body symbolizes emotion and the right side symbolizes reason. An axe in the upper left hand and a lotus in the upper right hand signify that in order to attain spiritual perfection, one should cut worldly attachments and conquer emotions. This enables one to live in the world without being affected by earthly temptations, just as a lotus remains in water but is not affected by it. A tray of *laddus* (a popular Indian sweet) near Ganesha denotes that he bestows wealth and prosperity upon his devotees. The lower right hand is shown in a blessing pose, which signifies that Ganesha always blesses his devotees.

A human body with a big belly

The human body possesses a human heart, which is a symbol of kindness and compassion toward all. Ganesha's body is usually portrayed wearing red and yellow clothes. Yellow symbolizes purity, peace and truthfulness and red symbolizes the activity in the world. These are the qualities of a perfect person who performs all duties in

Ganesha

the world, with purity, peace, and truthfulness. The big belly signifies that a perfect individual must have a large capacity to face all pleasant and unpleasant experiences of the world.

A mouse sitting near the feet of Ganesha and gazing at the tray of Laddus

A mouse symbolizes the ego that can nibble all that is good and noble in a person. A mouse sitting near the feet of Ganesha indicates that a perfect person is one who has conquered his (or her) ego. The mouse gazing at the *laddus*, but not eating them, denotes that a purified or controlled ego can live in the world without being affected by the worldly temptations. The mouse is also the vehicle of Ganesha, signifying that one must control ego in order for wisdom to shine forth.

Right foot dangling over the left foot

As stated above, the left side of the body symbolizes emotion and the right side symbolizes reason and knowledge. The right foot dangling over the left foot illustrates that in order to live a successful life one should utilize knowledge and reason to overcome emotions.

Durga.

Goddess Durga

The Sanskrit word *durga* means a fort or a place that is protected and thus difficult to reach. The goddess Durga protects mankind from evil and misery by destroying evil forces, such as selfishness, jealousy, prejudice, hatred, anger, and ego.

The worship of Durga is popular among Hindus. She is also called by other names, such as Divine Mother, Parvati, Ambika and Kali. In the form of Parvati, she is known as the divine spouse of Shiva and is the mother of her two sons, Ganesha and Karttikeya, and daughter Jyoti. There are many temples dedicated to Durga's worship in India.

In her images (see Figure 8), Durga is shown in female form, wearing red clothes. She has eighteen arms carrying many objects in her hands. The red colour symbolizes action and the red clothes signify that she is always busy destroying evil and protecting mankind from pain and suffering caused by evil forces.

A tiger symbolizes unlimited power. Durga riding a tiger indicates that she possesses unlimited power and uses it to protect virtue and destroy evil. The eighteen arms of Durga signify that she possesses combined power of the nine incarnations (symbolized by eighteen arms) of Vishnu that have appeared on the Earth at different times in the past.

The tenth incarnation, the Kalkin (a warrior king on a white horse), is still to come. Thus, Durga represents a united front of all divine forces against the negative forces of evil and wickedness.

The sound that emanates from a conch is the sound of the sacred syllable *OM* or *AUM* (see illustration above) which Hindus believe to be the original sound of creation. A conch in one of the goddess's hands signifies the ultimate victory of virtue over evil and righteousness over unrighteousness.

Other weapons in the hands of Durga such as a mace, sword, disc, arrow and trident convey the idea that one weapon cannot destroy all different kinds of enemies. Different weapons must be used to fight enemies depending upon the circumstances. For example, selfishness must be destroyed by detachment, jealousy by desirelessness, prejudice by self-knowledge, and ego by discrimination.

Shiva

Shiva represents the aspect of the supreme being (Brahman of the Upanishads) that continuously dissolves to recreate in the cyclic process of creation, preservation, dissolution and recreation of the universe.

Owing to his cosmic activity of dissolution and recreation, the words destroyer and destruction have been erroneously associated with Shiva. This difficulty arises when people fail to grasp the true significance of his cosmic role. The creation sustains itself by a delicate balance between the opposing forces of good and evil. When this balance is disturbed and sustenance of life becomes impossible, Shiva dissolves the universe for creation of the next cycle so that the unliberated souls will have another opportunity to liberate themselves from bondage with the physical world. Thus, Shiva protects the souls from pain and suffering, that would be caused by a dysfunctional universe. In analogous cyclic processes, winter is essential for spring to appear and the night is necessary for the morning to follow. To further illustrate, a goldsmith does not destroy gold when he melts old irreparable golden jewellery to create beautiful new ornaments.

Shiva is the lord of mercy and compassion. He protects devotees from evil forces such as lust, greed, and anger. He grants boons, bestows grace and awakens wisdom in his devotees. The symbolism discussed below includes only major symbols, which are common to all images and icons of Shiva venerated by Hindus. Since the tasks of Shiva are

Shiva.

numerous, he cannot be symbolized in one form. For this reason the images of Shiva vary significantly in their symbolism.

The unclad body covered with ashes

The unclad body symbolizes the transcendental aspect of Shiva. Since most things reduce to ashes when burned, ashes symbolize the physical universe. The ashes on the unclad body of Shiva signify that he is the source of the entire universe, which emanates from him, but He transcends the physical phenomena and is not affected by it.

Matted locks

Shiva is the master of yoga. The three matted locks on his head convey the idea that integration of the physical, mental and spiritual energies is the ideal of yoga.

Ganga

Ganga (the River Ganges) is associated with Hindu mythology and is the most sacred river of Hindus in India. Tradition says that one who bathes in Ganga (revered as Mother Ganga) in accordance with customary rites and ceremonies on religious occasions, in combination with certain astrological events, is freed from sin and attains knowledge, purity and peace. Ganga symbolically represented on the head of Shiva by a female (Mother Ganga) with a jet of water emanating from her mouth and falling on the ground, signifies that

Shiva destroys sin, removes ignorance, and bestows knowledge, purity and peace on the devotees.

The crescent moon

This is shown on the side of Shiva's head as an ornament, and not as an integral part of his countenance. The waxing and waning phenomenon of the moon symbolizes the time cycle through which creation evolves from beginning to end. Since Shiva is the eternal reality, He is beyond time. Thus, the crescent moon is only one of His ornaments, and not an integral part of him.

Three eyes

Shiva, also called *Tryambaka Deva* (literally, 'Three-eyed Lord'), is depicted as having three eyes: the sun is His right eye, the moon the left eye and fire the third eye. The two eyes on the right and left indicate his activity in the physical world. The third eye in the centre of the forehead symbolizes spiritual knowledge and power, and is thus called the eye of wisdom or knowledge. Like fire, the powerful gaze of Shiva's third eye annihilates evil, and thus the evildoers fear his third eye.

Half-open eyes

When Shiva opens his eyes, a new cycle of creation emerges and when he closes them, the universe dissolves for creation of the next cycle. Shiva's half-open eyes convey the idea that creation is going through cyclic process, with no absolute beginning or end. Shiva is the master of yoga, as he uses his yogic power to project the universe from himself. The half-open eyes also symbolize Shiva's yogic posture.

Kundalas (two ear rings)

Two *kundalas*, *alakshya* (meaning 'which cannot be shown by any sign') and *niranjan* (meaning 'which cannot be seen by mortal eyes') in the ears of Shiva signify that he is beyond ordinary perception. Since the *kundala* in the left ear of Shiva is of the type used by women and the one in his right ear is of the type used by men, these *kundalas* also symbolize Shiva and Shakti, male and female principles of creation.

Snake around the neck

Sages have used snakes to symbolize the yogic power of Shiva with which he dissolves and recreates the universe. Like a yogi, a snake hoards nothing, carries nothing, builds nothing, lives on air alone for a long time, and lives in mountains and forests. The venom of a snake, therefore, symbolizes the yogic power.

Snake (Vasuki Naga)

A snake is shown curled three times around the neck of Shiva and is looking towards his right side. The three coils of the snake symbolize the past, present and future time in cycles. Shiva wearing the curled snake like an ornament signifies that creation proceeds in cycles and is time dependent, but Shiva himself transcends time. The right side of the body symbolizes the human activities based upon knowledge, reason and logic. The snake looking towards Shiva's right side signifies that his eternal laws of reason and justice preserve the natural order in the universe.

Rudraksha necklace

Rudra is another name of Shiva. *Rudra* also means 'strict or uncompromising' and a*ksha* means, 'eye.' The *rudraksha* necklace worn by Shiva illustrates that he uses his cosmic laws firmly (i.e. without compromise) to maintain law and order in the universe. The necklace has 108 beads, which symbolize the elements used in the creation of the universe.

Varda Mudra

Shiva's right hand is shown in a boon-bestowing and blessing pose. As stated earlier, Shiva annihilates evil, grants boons, bestows grace, destroys ignorance, and awakens wisdom in his devotees.

Trident (trisula)

A three-pronged trident shown adjacent to Shiva symbolizes his three fundamental powers (*shakti*): will (*iccha*), action (*kriya*) and knowledge (*jnana*). The trident also symbolizes Shiva's power to destroy evil and ignorance.

Damaru (drum)

A small drum with two sides separated from each other by a thin neck-like structure (*damaru*) symbolizes the two utterly dissimilar states of existence, unmanifest and manifest. When a *damaru* is vibrated, it produces dissimilar sounds, which are fused together by resonance to create one sound. The sound thus produced symbolizes *nada*, the cosmic sound of AUM, which can be heard during deep meditation. According to Hindu scriptures, *nada* is the source of creation.

Kamandalu

A water pot (*kamandalu*) made from a dry pumpkin contains nectar and is shown on the ground next to Shiva. Yogis and ascetics use *kamandalu* to store clean water for drinking. The process of making *kamandalu* has deep spiritual significance. A ripe pumpkin is plucked from a plant, its fruit is removed and the shell is cleaned for containing the water. A ripe pumpkin symbolizes a spiritual seeker. The seed of the pumpkin represents the ego, cleaning of the pumpkin shell symbolizes surrendering the ego, and clean water symbolizes self-realization. In the same way a *kamandalu* is made from a pumpkin, an individual must clean his mind, i.e. give up the egoistic desires in order to experience the bliss of the higher self.

Nandi

The bull, *nandi*, is Shiva's vehicle. A bull symbolizes both power and ignorance. Shiva's use of the bull as a vehicle illustrates the idea that he removes ignorance and bestows power of wisdom on his devotees. The bull is called Vrisha in Sanskrit. Vrisha also means *dharma* (righteousness). Thus a bull shown next to Shiva also indicates that Shiva is the eternal companion of righteousness.

Tiger skin

A tiger skin symbolizes potential energy. Shiva, sitting on (or wearing) a tiger skin conveys the idea that he is the source of creative energy that remains in potential form during the dissolution state of the universe. Of his own divine will, Shiva activates the potential form of the creative energy to project the dynamic universe in endless cycles.

Cremation ground

Shiva sitting in the cremation ground signifies that he is the controller of death in the physical world. Since birth and death are cyclic, controlling the one implies controlling the other. Thus, Shiva is revered as the ultimate controller of birth and death in the phenomenal world.

Radha Krishna

Radha Krishna appear together, representing the male and female aspects of God, as the embodiment of love absolute. For the Vaishnava tradition, Krishna is the supreme personality of Godhead.

In popular images and pictures, Krishna stands in a relaxed pose with his weight supported on his left leg, his right foot casually crossed in front, his arms raised to hold his flute which he is playing, and his head is tilted playfully to one side. He wears a yellow dhoti, a flowing shawl, a garland of forest flowers, and ornaments lovingly offered to him by his devotees. In his long black hair is a peacock feather and jewelled crown. Beside him on his left stands Radharani, the personification of love and devotion. Her pose is shy and enchanting. Her dress is that of a cowherd girl, a simple skirt and blouse, and a veil lightly falling from her hair. She also wears a garland and jewelled ornaments. Her right hand is raised towards the devotees in the form of blessing, and her left hand holds a flower to offer to Krishna.

The popular posture of Krishna, as depicted above, illustrates that he has no work to perform. He simply engages in the dance of love with his devotees, attracting their minds from the material world to a dimension of love absolute, beyond duality of the mind. He plays his flute from which emanates the sound which is the seed of material creation and also the sound which once it impinges in the heart attracts all souls back to him.

Polytheism, monotheism and Hinduism

Owing to the ancient tradition of deity worship in Hinduism, many non-Hindus have a tendency to classify Hinduism as a polytheistic tradition. Some Hindus have an equally manifest tendency to classify their religion as a monotheistic tradition. Both these classifications are incorrect. Hinduism is neither polytheistic, nor monotheistic. Hindu deities are not independent or distinct gods or goddesses. They are various aspects (or different names and forms) of *Saguna Brahm*, the Ultimate Reality (God of other religions). Thus Hinduism cannot be equated with polytheism. The word monotheism arose from Western philosophy and represents the doctrine that there is but one God. Implicit in this doctrine is the belief that God is separate from his creation and that he has created the universe from nothing. Hindus believe in one ultimate reality, but do not subscribe to the idea that universe is created out of nothing. Hindu scriptures declare that non-existence cannot be the source of existence. Thus, the word monotheism is not broad enough to capture the fullness of Hindu religious thought.

There are three religious systems in Hinduism which more or less cover all popular schools of Hindu theology. The first of these is *advaita vedanta* (monism or non-dualism), as expounded by Adi Shankaracharya. The second is *vishishtadvaita* (qualified monism), taught by Ramanujacharya. The third is *dvaita* (dualism), taught by Madhavacharya. All these schools are based upon teachings of the Upanishads, as interpreted by their founders. *Advaita* maintains that *brahman* is the only absolute reality free from any internal or external distinctions, and individual selves and material objects are appearances made possible by operation of the magical power called *maya* (see Chapter 21). Thus *advaita* presents a pure monistic thought that goes as far back as the Rigveda, in which numerous hymns speak of one eternal being that 'breathed without breath,' and self-projected into the cosmic existence.

Vishishtadvaita also admits that *brahman* is the only absolute and independent reality and free from external distinctions, but maintains that individual selves and matter are his internal parts. Thus, Vishishtadvaita represents qualified-monism by declaring that *brahman* is the unity qualified by many internal parts or attributes. *Dvaita* declares that there are two categories of the ultimate reality. *Brahman* as personal God is the absolute reality and the individual selves and the material objects are the relative realities, distinct from each other, but dependent upon God. All these three systems maintain that there is only one ultimate reality, however they differ in their views on the relationships between the reality, individual selves and the cosmos. Thus Hinduism is a one-reality (or one-God) religion with the difference that the one reality (or God) is worshipped in different forms and by different names.

Hinduism comprises four principal denominations: Saivism, Shaktism, Vaishnavism and Smartism, who all worship one supreme being, though by different names. For Vaishnavites, Vishnu is the ultimate reality (God). For Saivites, the ultimate reality is Siva. For Shaktas, the ultimate reality is the goddess Shakti, and for the Smartas the choice of deity is left to the devotee.

Thus Hindu religious tradition cannot be captured by the classification of the monotheistic and polytheistic categories, because this classification ignores the reality as a whole and is focused on only one category called God. Hinduism views the reality as a whole i.e. a 'world-God-man doctrine', which describes God, soul and world (Sanskrit: *Pati pasu pasa*) as an integrated and inseparable unity.

The Hindu psyche

The Hindu psyche intuitively venerates the entire existence (celestial, physical, vegetable, animal and human) as sacred. To a Hindu the unfathomable infinite space, the home of glittering planets, that permeates the whole universe, including the interstices in human, animal and vegetable anatomies, is a deity. It contains the original sound of creation and is the abode of other deities such as the sun, the moon, the stars, the Milky Way and the deities of the dawn and the dusk. The air, which fills the space and sustains the respiratory systems of all creatures, is also a great deity. She remains mostly invisible, but manifests now and then as raging storms and tsunamis, heaving winds and cool breezes.

The Mother Earth that nourishes all God's creatures is also a great deity. She is never tired of giving us food, fruits and flowers, plants and vegetables, and providing us herbs to remedy our sick bodies. She is a symbol of forgiveness (we always trample her with our feet) and forbearance. The water, which is transparent blue in oceans, crystal clear in the lakes and brooks, dressed in white when resting on the peaks of the mountains, and pours down as rain from the dancing clouds in the skies, is a great deity. It nourishes our crops, becomes sap in the plants and vegetables and circulates as red blood in the veins of men and animals. It sustains our lives, washes our dirt and quenches our thirst.

The fire, which blazes in the sun, which dances in every kitchen, and which sleeps in all fuels, is also a great deity. It shines in the stars, lends vision to every eye, and sustains our metabolism as vital heat, without which we cannot even exist. In the form of the sacred fire during religious rites and ceremonies, it represents all the deities and invokes their presence.

The birds and animals are also sacred, since they are the vehicles of Hindu deities. The lion is the vehicle of Durga, the bull that of Shiva, the swan that of Saraswati, the mouse that of Ganesha, the owl that of Lakshmi, and the Garuda that of Vishnu. The horse pulls the chariot of Indra as well as that of the sun. The snake is also sacred as Shiva wears him as an ornament and Vishnu rests on him, and the cow, which provides milk to the child like a mother, is the sacred above all, a deity *par excellence*. Nearer home, the mother is a deity, the father is a deity, and every elder is a deity. The teacher who gives us knowledge is a deity, the guest who comes to our home is a deity, and the king who protects us is a deity.

The roster of Hindu deities is thus endless. The Hindu psyche has always harboured a deep sense of sanctity towards all elements and forces of nature in their all forms. What is more significant about the

51

Hindu psyche is that it looks at everything in nature as having life and consciousness. With this reverential attitude towards all forms of life, the Hindu sees inanimate becoming animate, unconscious becoming conscious, thoughtless becoming thoughtful, insensitive becoming sensitive, and inactive becoming active.

Chapter 4

The Hindu View of the Universe

> A human being is part of the whole, called by us
> *Universe*; a part limited in time and space. He
> experiences himself, his thoughts and feelings as
> something separated from the rest – a kind of optical
> delusion of his consciousness. This delusion is a kind of
> prison for us, restricting us to our personal desires and
> to affection for a few persons nearest us. Our task must
> be to free ourselves from this prison by widening our
> circle of compassion to embrace all living creatures and
> the whole of nature in its beauty. Nobody is able to
> achieve this completely but the striving for such
> achievement is, in itself, a part of the liberation and a
> foundation for inner security.
>
> Albert Einstein (Einstein 1930)

If we ask 'What is the source of this universe?' we encounter two popular theories. One is the theory of creation and the other the theory of projection or manifestation. The former suggests that God created the universe. The latter advocates the view that the universe emanates from the cosmic Absolute in perpetual cycles of creation, dissolution and recreation. According to the theory of creation, God is the 'efficient cause' (agent of creation or change) of the universe, but this theory does not address the material cause. According to the theory of manifestation, the cosmic Absolute is both the agent of creation, as well as the material cause of the universe. Creation implies something coming out of nothing or non-existence becoming existence. The Upanishads declare that something cannot come out of nothing and non-existence cannot be the source of existence. The theory of creation further assumes that God must have been sleeping or resting and suddenly it occurred to Him that He should have company. The idea of a lonely God, sleeping God or God needing rest is not accepted in Hinduism.

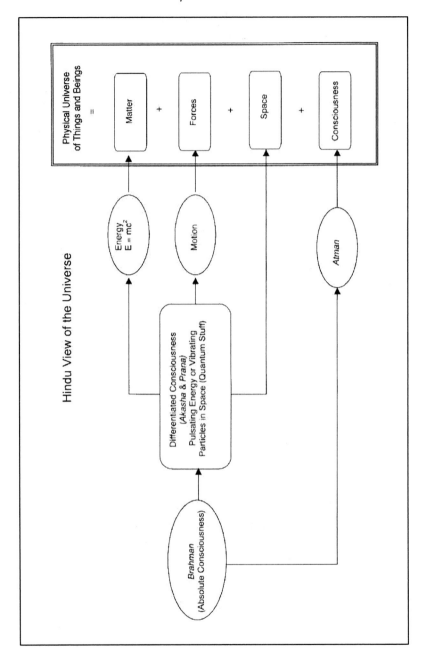

Figure 4. The Hindu view of the universe.

The theory of manifestation puts forth two possibilities: either the whole of God has transformed into the universe or only a part of Him is transformed into the cosmos. If the whole of God is transformed, then there is no God beyond the cosmos. This idea limits the potentiality of God and is thus viewed as an absurd hypothesis in Hinduism. The only view that does not put theological limits on God and satisfies the rational mind is that God is both transcendent as well as immanent. The Isa Upanishad says, *'Poornam-adah, poornam-idam, poornath-poornam udachyate. Poor-nasya poornam-adaya, poornam-eva-va-sishyate'* (Isa-U 1) meaning 'That [un-manifest] is Whole. This [manifest] is Whole. From that Whole comes forth this Whole. From that Whole when this Whole is subtracted, what remains again is Whole.' The Upanishad says, 'The whole universe is a manifestation and product of that universal, formless, and causeless Being. The sun, the moon and all the quarters, all knowledge, and the souls of all existing beings are parts and manifestations of that single all-immanent Being.' (Mun-U 2.1, 4–5)

Mathematically, 'Brahman – Universe = Brahman', or 'infinity minus infinity equals infinity'. This verse of the Upanishad expresses the mystery of creation, i.e. this universe comes forth from the Divine, yet the universe takes nothing from the Divine and adds nothing to It. Divine remains ever the same. Since the universe has come forth from the Divine, Hindus maintain that all things and beings are sacred and must be treated so in human thought and action. This is one of the fundamental tenets of Hinduism.

In the Hindu view, the world we live in and perceive by our senses is a projection of the cosmic whole, called *brahman* by the seers of the Upanishads. 'Out of the seed there evolves that which is already in the seed, pre-existent in being, predestined in its will to become, prearranged in the delight of becoming,' writes Sri Aurobindo (Aurobindo 1985:134). The Sanskrit word for arising of the universe from *brahman* is *srishti,* which means 'projection' and not 'creation'. The Upanishad says 'Brahman is the whole universe. Heaven, Earth, and sky, together with mind and life-breath are all centred in Him. Dismiss all other explanations. He is the one and only Existence. This knowledge is the bridge to immortality.' (Mun-U 2.2, 5)

The Hindu view takes special care to emphasize that the immanence of God does not mean identity of God with the universe. Hindu sages maintain that the physical universe and its laws constitute the process by which the divinity at rest (transcendental or unmanifest reality) becomes divinity in motion (immanent or manifest reality).

The same view is expressed in Buddha's historic words 'Nirvana, [the ultimate reality] is samsara, [the physical world], and samsara is Nirvana.' By the process of manifestation, the unknown becomes known, invisible becomes visible, and infinite and undivided appears finite and divided into things and beings of the universe. The universe is the process by which the Self surveys Itself, through the human body, mind and matter. In the words of Deepak Chopra:

> The source of all creation is divinity (or the Spirit); the process of creation is divinity in motion (or the mind); and the object of creation is the physical universe (which includes the physical body). These three components of Reality – Spirit, mind and body, or observer, the process of observing, and the observed – are essentially the same thing. They all come from the same place: the field of pure potentiality which is pure unmanifest.

(Chopra 1997:4)

According to the Taittiriya Upanishad 2.1, in the beginning the universe arises from Brahman in the form of *akasha* (space) and *prana* (force) (*see* Figure 4), which together give rise to all animate and inanimate objects of the universe. *Akasha* and *prana* also give rise to air, fire (i.e. sunlight), earth and water, which together support the life on Earth. The Sanskrit word *akash* is generally translated as space, but it doesn't mean empty space. *Akash* represents the infinite space containing the primal energy (called *shakti* or *prakriti* in Sanskrit). The Sanskrit word *prana* is generally translated as force, but actually means divine vibrations or pulsations (*spanda* in Sanskrit). *Prana* manifests as physical force in matter and life force in human and other beings. The process of manifestation sets the primal energy in motion (similar to the 'Big Bang' theory of modern physics) at the beginning of the universe. Hindu scriptures say, "Everything in this universe has been projected, *prana* vibrating." *Akasha* and *prana* constitute the vibrating primal energy, which results in the dynamic nature of the universe.

Modern science has revealed that, in the words of Fritjof Capra:

> the constituents of atoms, the subatomic particles, are dynamic patterns which do not exist as isolated entities, but as integral parts of an inseparable network of

interactions. These interactions involve a ceaseless flow of energy manifesting itself as the exchange of particles; a dynamic interplay in which particles are created and destroyed without end in a continual variation of energy patterns. The particle interactions give rise to the stable structures, which build up the material world, which again do not remain static, but oscillate in rhythmic movements. The whole universe is thus engaged in endless motion and activity; in a continual cosmic dance of energy.

(Capra 1984: 184)

In the Bhagavad Gita 3.24, Sri Krishna refers to the endless activity of the divine energy in the following words, 'If I did not engage in action, these worlds would perish.'

According to David Böhm (1917–94, one of the foremost quantum physicists of his generation), there is the 'implicate' and the 'explicate' order in nature. What Hindu scriptures call *brahman*, Böhm calls the *implicate* order, and what Hindus call samsara, Böhm calls the *explicate* order. The implicate order, as Böhm explains, is the unbroken undifferentiated wholeness in which there are no differences or distinctions, and where everything is connected to everything else. At the implicate level everything is made of the same substance. The explicate order is the world of objects with name and form, which we perceive with our mind and the senses. At the explicate level, a plant or a tree is seen different from an animal, and a man is perceived distinct from everything else. At the implicate level, all matter, whether here on Earth or in outer space, is involved in the eternal dance of energy, in which particles are created, destroyed, and recreated in an endless network of interactions. At the explicate level, the dance of creation and destruction goes on through the daily rhythm of birth, death, and rebirth.

In the Hindu view, the universe projects from and dissolves back into Brahman in endless cycles. The expansion (i.e. projection) and the contraction (i.e. dissolution) of the universe are called *lila* (the divine sport) in Hindu scriptures. In this divine play, the One becomes many and the many return into the One in an endless rhythmic fashion symbolized by the cosmic Dance of Shiva. In the words of Swami Vivekananda:

Shiva as Nataraja (Sanskrit for 'Lord of the Dance').
Shiva's dance symbolizes God's endless dance of creation,
preservation, dissolution and recreation.

The whole of this nature exists, it becomes finer,
subsides; and then after a period of rest, as it were, and
the whole universe is again projected forward. The
same combination, the same evolution, the same
manifestations appear and remain playing, as it were for
a certain time, only to become finer and finer, until the
entire physical phenomena subsides, and again comes

out. Thus it goes on backwards and forwards with a wave-like motion throughout eternity. Time, space, and causation are all within this nature.

(Vivekananda Complete Works Vol. 2)

In the Bhagavad Gita, Sri Krishna describes this rhythmic play of creation, 'At the end of a *kalpa* [time cycle], all beings return to my *prakriti* [nature]. At the beginning of another *kalpa*, I send them forth again.' (BG 3, 24)   There are numerous creation metaphors, myths, and legends that exist side-by-side in Hinduism.   However, the underlying message of all these stories and legends is always the same, i.e. the universe projects from and dissolves back into *brahman* in endless cycles.   Scripture says, 'The Divine Being like a sea surges upward in a wave of creation, then subsides again into its own nature. Waves of universes rise incessantly, in infinite numbers one after another.' (Yoga Vasishtha 2.19)   A popular Vedic verse, the Purusha Sukta (RV 10.90,1–2), describes the projection of the universe by the Supreme Being as a divine sacrifice.

The Hindu view of the expanding and contracting universe has a parallel in modern science. As Fritjof Capra explains:

> Einstein's equations do not provide a unique answer [to the question of the expanding universe]… Some models predict that the expansion will continue forever; according to others, it is slowing down and will eventually change into a contraction. These models describe an oscillating universe, expanding for billions of years then contracting until its total mass has condensed into a small ball of matter, and then expanding again, and so on without end… experiencing the universe as an organic and rhythmically moving cosmos. The Hindus were able to develop evolutionary cosmologies which come very close to our modern scientific models.

(Capra 1984: 184)

The following is the popular *Hymn of Creation* in the Rig Veda, which comprises seven verses and describes the mystery of creation:

> Existence or non-existence was not then. Neither was the Earth, nor the sky, nor the great space beyond. What covered it? Where was it? What gave shelter? Was there cosmic water unfathomable and deep?

Death or immortality was not then. Undistinguished
were night and day. By itself, that One breathed
without the air. Other than That nothing did exist.

Darkness there was concealed by darkness.
Undistinguished all this was one water. Covered by
nothing, that One emerged and became creative by the
power of its own contemplation.

Thereafter rose desire in the beginning, desire, the
primal seed and germ of Spirit. The sages who have
searched their hearts with wisdom know that which is,
is kin to that which is not.

And they have stretched their cord across the void, and
know what was above, and what below. Seminal
powers made fertile mighty forces. Below was strength,
and over it was impulse.

But, after all, who knows, and who can say whence it
all came, and how creation happened? The gods
themselves are later than creation, so who knows truly
whence it has arisen?

He, the first origin of this creation, whether he formed it
all or did not form it. He, who surveys it all from
highest heaven, he verily knows it, or perhaps he knows
not.

(RV 10.129,1–7)

The above hymn affirms the Vedic view that the manifest universe
arose from the unmanifest, which did not create life but became life.
The universe in this sense is the development of that which already
exists and not the bringing into being of that which is non-existent. All
things and beings of the world have evolved from *brahman* through the
process of manifestation. Nothing new was created during this
process, only transformation took place from non-being to being, or
unmanifest to manifest. The last four words, 'perhaps he knows not',
of the *Hymn of Creation* above are significant, because they point out
uncertainty in human knowledge and have given rise to the Hindu
tradition of respect for other religious ideas and its important doctrine
of universal tolerance and acceptance.

In conclusion, the basic world-view developed by the Vedic seers,
based upon their spiritual (non-intellectual) experience, is consistent

with the findings of modern science. The Vedic view is that all things and beings of the universe are inseparable and interdependent parts of the ultimate reality, *brahman.* "Just as the potentiality of a seed brings forth a tree, so also the potentiality of Brahman brings forth the universe, " says Swami Sivananda. (Sivananda 1997: 80).

The unity of *brahman* and the physical phenomena may be compared to the unity of all different objects such as a hill, a forest, a valley, a shepherd, a river and the landscape of a beautiful painting, which are all made of one substance, the canvas. Just as the canvas appears in different forms and is called by different names in the painting, *brahman*, the pure consciousness, manifests itself not only as sentient beings, but also as insentient objects.

Chapter 5

The Hindu View of the Individual

> Above the senses is the mind. Above the mind is the
> intellect. Above the intellect is the ego. Above the ego is
> the unmanifested seed, the Primal Cause (atman).
>
> Katha Upanishad 1.3,10-11

According to Hindu scriptures, an individual is in reality the atman (individual self) dressed in a physical body. What is this atman? The Bhagavad Gita 2,20 answers, 'The atman is neither born nor does it die. It does not cease to be after it comes into being. Unborn, eternal, constant and ancient, it does not die when the body perishes at death.' The Upanishad illustrates functioning of atman in the human body in the famous metaphor, "Know that the atman is the rider, the body the chariot, the intellect the charioteer, and the mind the reins. The senses, say the wise, are the horses; the roads they travel are the mountains of desire. The wise call the Self the enjoyer, when it is united with the body, mind and the senses." (Kat-U 1.3, 3)

The Sanskrit word *atman*, meaning 'God within' is the inner essence of a human being. Just as the electricity illumines a glass bulb and produces light, the atman in the human body illumines the body and generates consciousness, which in turn gives rise to the mind. Without the atman the human mind cannot exist and the human body would be a corpse. To use a metaphor, if we imagine the human being to be a computer, the body the hardware, the mind the software, the electricity (that operates both the hardware and the software) would be the atman.

The human body is made of the gross matter and the mind of the subtle matter (energy), but the atman is immaterial or the spiritual reality. Since the atman is not made of matter, it is not subject to the law of causation. The atman is beyond time and space and thus beyond the death and decay.

The Upanishads teach that the inner essence of all things and beings is *brahman*, the ultimate reality. Atman is the manifestation of *brahman* in the human body. The central theme of the Upanishads is that in the liberated state the atman is identical with *brahman*. This truth is reflected in the famous Upanishadic statement, '*Tat Tvam Assi*,' meaning 'Thou art That.' (Chan-U 6.9, 3)

The word atman is generally translated as soul, self or spirit. However, in view of the Western definition of the soul, atman and soul are not the same. What westerners call soul, Hindus call *chitta* (or *sukhsma sharira*), the subtle or astral body. In the western view, the soul is created by God. In the Hindu view, the atman, being eternal, is not created by God. It is a part of God. If it were created by God, it would have a beginning and subsequently an end, because whatever has a beginning must have an end. Only what is beginningless will be endless, i.e. immortal and eternal. If God is likened to the infinite fire, the atman is the eternal spark of that infinite fire. If God is likened to the infinite ocean, the atman is a drop of water of that eternal ocean. Being a part of God, the atman is pure, divine, and immortal. The Bhagavad Gita 2,24 says that the atman is 'Beyond the power of the sword and fire, beyond the power of the waters and winds, this atman is everlasting, omnipresent, unchangeable, immovable, and everlasting.' The light of the atman in the physical body is the thought 'I am', the individual consciousness.

The 'I am' or the individual consciousness enables one to think, feel, imagine, conceptualize and respond to stimuli. Without this consciousness, one cannot function as an individual. The human consciousness is impersonal. One may say, 'I am conscious,' but no one says, 'my consciousness'. Since we all first say, 'I am... ', and then say whatever other name we may have, all human beings are spiritually united through this 'I am'. This impersonal consciousness is present in all human bodies and is the common denominator of human existence. However, when it identifies with a particular human body and says, 'I am so and so,' the individuality comes into picture. Hindu scriptures maintain that what actually dwells in the human body is the atman. The reflection of the atman in the human heart gives rise to 'I am', which is the individual consciousness and is called by other names such as the conditioned self and *jivatman*. The mind and the senses are the content of this conditioned consciousness.

During the waking state, the atman uses the mind and senses as instruments to interact with the physical world. During the dream state, the atman uses the mind alone as an instrument and creates a different world (the dream world). During the deep sleep state, the mind dissolves and the atman remains in its original state of peace and happiness, but its bondage with the physical world remains in the seed form. The Upanishads compare the mind with the moon. The moon has no light of its own and shines only because of the reflected light of the sun. Likewise, the mind has no consciousness of its own and functions only with the reflected consciousness of the atman.

The mind cannot reach the atman, much less define or conceptualize it. The mind is a limited tool, whereas the atman is infinitely conscious, infinitely alive, infinitely blissful, and infinitely free. This being the case, why do we die, why do we commit evil, and why do we feel weak and limited?

As far as death is concerned, atman does not die, only the body dies. We know that the sun does not move; yet we speak of the sunset and sunrise, which actually are caused by the movement of the Earth and not of the sun. So too the atman shines constantly and birth and death happen to the physical body alone. Upon death of the body, the atman departs encased in its astral body and enters the astral world (*see* Chapter 13). If the atman has not attained moksha (liberation or spiritual perfection) during its life on Earth, it will be born again and again until it attains eternal freedom from physical limitations.

Why do we commit evil? We commit evil because we have mistakenly identified ourselves with the ego (the false self or the little self) and not with the true self (atman). Because of this wrong identification, we cling on to egoistic thought of 'me and mine'. Sages tell us that this 'me and mine' is the root cause of all evil in the world. Identification with the ego causes an intense desire to control things, restlessness, passion for external power, struggle for approval by others and fear of loss of acquired power and possessions. Identification with the atman, on the other hand, removes fear, bestows peace and happiness, and there is no compulsion to control, no intense desire for external power or struggle for approval by others.

We feel miserable and limited because of wrong upbringing, religious dogma, superstitions and wrong notions of ourselves. We fail to realize that the kingdom of heaven is not of this world, but is within us. Instead of reminding ourselves of our divine nature, we call ourselves miserable sinners. Man is a lion, but lives and acts like a sheep, says Swami Vivekananda, who explains man's sheepish conduct through the following metaphorical tale.

A pregnant lioness was in search of a prey when she noticed a flock of sheep. She jumped at one of them and in the process gave birth to a cub, but died herself on the spot. The cub was brought up in the flock of the sheep. He learned to eat grass and bleat like a sheep. He never knew that he was a lion. One day a forest lion was passing by the flock and was astonished to see a huge lion in the flock eating grass and bleating like a sheep. At the sight of the forest lion, the flock fled away and so did the lion-sheep. Next time the forest lion came again and found the lion-sheep asleep. He woke him up and said, 'You are a lion.' The lion-sheep said, 'No,' and began to bleat like a sheep. The forest lion took him to a nearby pond and asked him to look in the water at his own image and see if it resembled the forest lion. The lion-sheep looked in the water and acknowledged that his own image in the water looked like a lion. The forest lion began to roar and taught the lion-sheep to do the same. The lion-sheep did so and soon began roaring like a lion, and he was no longer a sheep.

Chapter 6

The Graded Nature of Hinduism

Hinduism is not a 'one-size-fits-all' type of a religion. Every mind is different. People do not go to the same school, study the same subject or obtain the same degree. There is diversity in nature and the mind being a part of the nature, rejoices in diversity. Why then should we impose our own beliefs on others, claiming them to be the greatest? The Hindu sages answered this question, several millennia ago, in a unanimous voice. Life is a long journey that has already begun, they proclaimed. Some are ahead and some are behind. Some are travelling faster than others, but all human beings are destined to reach the destination in this or a future life, depending upon their will, effort and perseverance. Hindu sages tell us that we move from lower to higher truth until the highest is attained. No religious belief is totally erroneous, although one may be less true than the other. As Dr Radhakrishnan observes, 'The deities of some men are in water (at bathing places), those of the more advanced are in the heavens, those of the children [in religion] are in images and icons of wood and stone, but the sage finds his God in his own self.' (Radhakrishnan 1926: 24)

Since the times immemorial, Hindus have recognized that the cosmic time is cyclic, that the present life is only one in a series of lives, and that men are in different stages of their journey. Thus Hinduism provides a religious discipline, which will suit the temperament, spiritual yearning, education and training in such a way that the seeker can advance from one stage to the next. Hinduism does not thrust everyone in the pigeonhole of one unalterable creed. It caters to the needs of the human mind in accordance with the Hindu doctrine of spiritual competence (*adhikara*). This doctrine states that religious discipline must be given in accordance with the spiritual competence of the individual. A labourer, whose heart hungers for concrete gods, needs a different type of religion than a scholar, who finds God everywhere. An active man finds his God in action, the man of feeling in his heart, the less evolved in signs and symbols, but the wise man finds Him everywhere.

Attribute	Popular Hinduism	Advanced Hinduism	Highest Religion
Belief in the nature of reality	Predominately dualistic	Dualistic in the beginning and monistic in the end	Predominately monistic
Deity	Incarnation of God or deity of the traditional Hindu pantheon (see Fig.3)	*Ishta-devta* (personal god)	Atman (Self)
Worship	*Puja*, temple worship, elaborate religious rites and rituals	*Puja*, yoga and meditation	Meditation
Scripture	Bhagavad Gita, Smritis	Bhagavad Gita, Vedas, Darshanas, Agamas, Tantras	Sruti
Religious interest	Biological values: Health, strength, vitality, power, possessions and pleasure, etc	Intellectual values: Knowledge, logic, reason, *ahimsa*, clarity, coherence, simplicity, etc	Spiritual Values: Intuitive knowledge, divine wisdom, *ahimsa*, love, renunciation, etc
Religious focus	Doing	Becoming	Being
Ethics	*Yama* and *niyama* to be practised	*Yama* and *niyama* to be practised	*Yama* and *niyama* are natural
Festivals and pilgrimages	Heavy emphasis	Moderate emphasis	Minor emphasis

Figure 5. The graded nature of Hinduism.

Another Hindu doctrine, the doctrine of *ishta devata*, requires that the worshipper should choose a form of the supreme being that suits his temperament and offer his devotion to the chosen deity (*ishta devata*) in prayer and meditation. The beliefs and practices of the Hindu religious tradition are thus graded in accordance with the spiritual competence of the human mind and form a 3-step spiritual ladder, as depicted in Figure 5.

Popular Hinduism

Popular Hinduism, the religion of the masses, generally reflects traditional ideas and attitudes based upon teachings of the *smritis* (secondary scriptures). The beliefs and practices enumerated in the Puranas (Hindu mythology) form the heart of the popular religion of Hindus. Almost everything one encounters in the religious life of the majority of Hindus represents popular Hinduism. The concept of God in popular Hinduism is predominantly theistic. God is worshipped in the form of incarnations, which are traditionally limited to ten. Religious rites and rituals are considered as purification acts, which move one towards God. Scriptural reading is generally limited to Bhagavad Gita, Epics and Puranas.

In Hindu culture, yoga and meditation is the way to God-discovery through self-discovery. Yoga purifies the body for meditation and meditation elevates human consciousness to God-consciousness. Yoga and meditation liberate the soul from physical limitations. However, at the popular level, yoga and meditation are not practiced seriously, since the masses are mostly interested in immediate enjoyment of the world and much less in the liberation of the atman. Yoga and meditation are popular only at advanced levels of Hinduism. Some Hindus at the popular level practice simple yogic exercises such as *asanas* and simple forms of meditation.

Advanced Hinduism

When the devotee's mind is purified through selfless action (*nishkama karma*) and made one-pointed by sincere worship (*upasana*), he begins to ask questions such as, 'Where has this universe come from?', 'Who am I?' and 'Why I am here?' Such questions develop deep desire for knowledge. The devotee approaches a spiritual teacher (guru), sits at his or her feet, tunes his mind to the knowledge imparted by the guru, and begins to absorb and practice the teachings. Why must the student sit at the teacher's feet? Just as water flows naturally from higher to lower level, sitting at the feet of the guru (which is symbolic of faith in the teacher and the seeker's remarkable desire for learning) allows natural flow of spiritual knowledge from the guru to the disciple. When students receive this knowledge directly from the guru, the students' ignorance of the true nature of the world and of their own self is destroyed and they begin to acquire true knowledge.

Advanced Hinduism is a religion of learning through yoga and meditation and beginning of the spiritual practice (*sadhana*) to help devotees realize their eternal or divine nature, which is pure awareness transcending the desire and duality. Here traditional worship, religious rites and rituals take the backseat. The primary goal is the spiritual *sadhana*, which opens the eye of intuition and helps the devotee to go beyond the intellect and ultimately experience the Self within.

The essence of the advanced religion is love of God, selfless service to others, pursuit of honesty, justice, goodness, decency, firm belief in reason and common sense. The advanced religion is not about preoccupation with rites and rituals, philosophical debates and discussions, theological ideas and ideologies, or deep involvement in organized religious activities. The advanced religion reflects kindness and compassion, desire for knowledge, and mental and emotional balance. The advanced religion is not for the masses, but for dedicated and sincere seekers, who choose a spiritual lifestyle and are willing and able to pursue the inquiry 'Who am I?'

Highest religion (spirituality)

Highest religion transforms human consciousness into divine consciousness through discipline, *tapas* (self-restraint), detachment, yoga and meditation. This is the religion of the saints and seers. A saint or a seer is one who has realized the atman, lives in the atman, knows the atman, and is one with the atman. He or she speaks of the atman and shows the way to the atman. Such a person is the living symbol of the highest religion and spirituality and true beneficiary of humanity. Such persons are free from I-ness and mine-ness, free from anger, lust and greed. They love all beings as their own Self. They are ever fearless and generous. Their nature is to give and not to take. They see the entire cosmos as the projection of their own Self. They possess divine wisdom and intuitive knowledge. Their spiritual vibrations purify the world. They are the only real lovers of humanity, because they feel the presence of God everywhere and in everyone.

The knowledge is the same for all sages and saints, but their lifestyles and conduct may be different. Sage Vasishtha was a *karma yogi.* Not only did he perform normal worldly activities, he was also an advisor to King Dasharatha. Raja Janaka was a great sage of his time and also a very popular king. On the other hand, sage Dattatreya was a wanderer and had no possessions. Paramahansa Ramakrishna, one of the greatest saints of the modern era, lived a normal life, championed the cause of religious tolerance and gave spiritual instruction to a large community of his disciples. Ramana Maharshi, another spiritual genius of the modern times, influenced the lives of numerous disciples from many countries with his spiritual power. Sages and saints have tremendous transforming effect on the lives of the people. The Bhagavad Gita 4,7 says that God incarnates as a sage or saint to restore righteousness (*dharma*), whenever righteousness is on the decline and unrighteousness (*adharma*) is on the rise.

Chapter 7

Karma and Rebirth

The belief in karma and transmigration of the soul is the most important component in the religious life of a Hindu, and a fundamental principle of Hindu consciousness. The Upanishad says, "Whoever longs for the objects of desire is born here or there to fulfil them. But one who has fulfilled all his desires is freed from the birth and death. To such a person, Self (*atman*) reveals its true nature – eternal life of peace and bliss." (Mundaka Upanishad 3.2, 2.) Hindus believe that the course of natural world is determined by operation of the immutable laws of nature. The Upanishad says, 'Verily O Gargi, at the command of that Imperishable the sun and the moon stand in their respective positions. At the command of that Imperishable, the heaven and the earth stand in their respective positions... some rivers flow to the east from the snowy mountains, others to the West and still others in whatever direction they flow...' (Brh-U 3.8, 9)

The word karma literally means 'deed or action and its consequence'. What distinguishes good karma from bad karma is the quality of thoughts, deeds or actions. Hindus maintain that by the quality of our thoughts and actions, we form our characters and shape our destinies. Our good deeds are not wasted; neither can we escape our bad deeds. According to Hindu scriptures, the same cosmic law that operates in the natural world as *rita* (the natural order in the universe) also operates in the realm of the human mind and morals as the Law of Karma. Karma is the force that keeps the soul tied to the physical existence. One of the definitions of moksha (spiritual freedom) is 'freedom from karma.'

What is the Law of Karma?

The doctrine of karma, the law of actions and their retribution, is really the law of causation as applied to the moral realm. Hindus view the Law of Karma as a universal law inherent in nature. The Vedic seers did not invent this law; they merely discovered it and helped us to

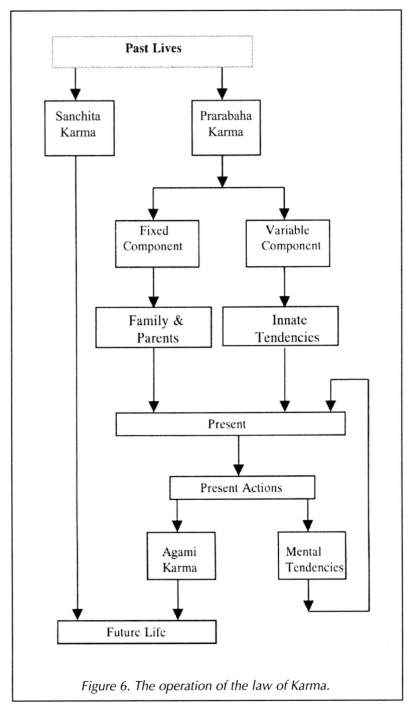

Figure 6. The operation of the law of Karma.

understand it. The law that every action has a reaction works in the scientific world as well as in the moral world. The nature of the effect is exactly like the nature of the cause. A bitter seed will bring forth a bitter fruit and vice versa. As the proverb goes, 'He who lives by the sword perishes by the sword, and he who lives by love of truth fosters love.' If we want to get the oranges, we have to plant the orange seeds. It can never happen that if we plant the orange seeds that we will get apples, or vice versa. The same idea is expressed in another traditional proverb: 'Plant the melons and reap the melons; plant the beans and reap the beans.' Whatsoever a man shall sow, that also shall he reap. This is what Hindus call the Law of Karma. Other popular expressions of the Law of Karma are: 'every action has an equal and opposite reaction,' 'you get what you pay for,' 'don't do to others what you don't want done to you,' 'as you sow, so shall you reap,' 'if you love, you will be loved; if you hate, you will be hated,' and 'what comes around goes around.'

According to the Law of Karma, every human action inevitably leads to results, good or bad, depending upon the moral quality of the deed. There is no such thing as action without results. The Law of Karma conserves the moral consequences of all actions, and conditions our present and/or future lives accordingly. In part, our present life is determined by the results of our past deeds. We are the effects of our own infinite past. Every child that is born in this world is born to work out its own past karma. The doctrine of karma says that the Day of Judgment is not in some remote future, but here and now, and none can escape it. Hindus maintain that the Law of Karma is a philosophical and spiritual necessity. It enjoys the philosophical advantage over the Western religious idea of eternal hell and heaven, because any reward or punishment of eternal duration can never be in proportion to one's deeds. In the absence of the Law of Karma, it would be impossible to think of an impartial God. If there were no personal accountability, eternal justice would be a meaningless idea.

How does the Law of Karma operate?

According to Hindu scriptures, every karma generates a vibrating force or subliminal inclinations (*vasanas* in Sanskrit), which get embedded in one's subconscious mind. The characteristics of these *vasanas* are such that like attracts like, or in other words, love attracts love and hatred attracts hatred. Each karma continues to attract until its energy in the form of subconscious impressions is exhausted. Hindu sages reveal that seeds of the past karma remain embedded in the subtle body (*see*

Chapter 13). A yogi can perceive the plasma of the subtle body through mystic vision and predict the natural tendencies or subconscious imprints (*samskaras*) of an individual. Yogis teach that some of the karmic seeds of one's past thoughts and actions are released into a person's nerve system in each lifetime, thus providing direction to the human personality. The effects of past actions are said to determine one's family and generate natural tendencies for the quality of life on Earth.

As shown in Figure 6, the past karma of an individual consists of two parts, *prarabdha karma* and *sanchita karma*. The *prarabdha karma* is the part of one's past karma, which is to bear fruit in the present life of the individual. The *sanchita karma* is the accumulated karma of the previous births, which is to bear fruit in the future. The karma, which is being done now will produce results in the future and is called the *agami karma* (other names are *kriyamana karma* and *vartamana karma*). In Hindu tradition, these three karmas are compared to an archer and his arrows. The arrows that have been shot by the archer, which are already on their way to the target and the archer has no control over them, are akin to the *prarabdha karma*. The arrows he is about to shoot are akin to the *agami karma* and the arrows lying in his quiver are akin to the *sanchit karma*. This illustrates the Hindu view that one has no control over *prarabdha karma*, but full control over *sanchit* and *agami* karma .

The *prarabdha karma* of an individual consists of two components: fixed and variable. The fixed component is beyond our control and consists of that component of the past karma which determines one's parents, the family, culture and the country in which a child must be born, the general features of the physical body that the child will eventually develop, and the social and religious environment in which the child must grow.

The variable component of the past karma remains latent in the subconscious mind of the child in the form of natural habits and tendencies (*samskaras*). It is this variable part of the past karma, containing the inherent tendencies for the quality of life on Earth, that can be controlled by training, education, initiative and free will. The level of success one can achieve in diluting the effects of the variable component of the past karma, however, depends upon the power of the *samskars*, the quality of the education and training the individual receives and the strength of the individual will.

Every human action, physical or mental, produces two effects. First, depending upon the moral quality of the action, appropriate fruits of the action will be rewarded later, either in the same life or in a future life. Second, the action leaves residual impressions (*samskaras*) on the subconscious mind of the individual. These *samskaras* generate thought waves (*vrittis*) and thereby determine the character of the individual. Thus, actions determine the personal conduct and this conduct moulds the character, in a revolving chain of cause and effect. A person becomes good by performing good deeds and evil by performing evil deeds, says Brhadaranyaka Upanishad 3. 2, 13. According to the science of yoga, the negative thought waves which arise in the human mind because of innate tendencies of past karma, can be neutralized by introducing positive thought waves generated by the human will. Upanishad says, "You are what your deep desire is. As is your desire, so is your will. As is your will, so is your deed. As is your deed, so is your destiny." (Brhadaranyaka Upanishad 4.4, 5)

When an apple falls from a tree, gravity causes the fall of the apple itself. However, not only the law of gravity, but also the law of conservation of energy, determines the consequences of this event. In just the same way, the overall consequences of human actions are determined by the doctrine of karma as well as the doctrine of free will. The negative *samskaras* of past karma can be overcome by human will. In the Hindu view, what separates a saint and a sinner is only time. With right knowledge and effort, a sinner of today can be a saint of tomorrow. 'The cards of life are given to us [in the form of samskaras], but we can play them as we wish, and win or lose, as we play,' writes Dr Radhakrishnan (Radhakrishnan 1926: 54). The Law of Karma has a parallel in physics. Just as the energy gained by a moving body is a function of the mass of the body and its velocity, the karma acquired by an individual is a function of the type of act and the goodwill or bad will put by the ego in the act itself.

When a crime is committed, two possibilities exist. Either the person is creating a brand new karma (*agami karma*) by misusing his free will, or his action is motivated by the negative *samskaras* of his past karma. In either case, he is fully responsible for his actions. He could have been helped if his free will had been strengthened by yoga, meditation, right education, right training, prayers, positive thinking, right environment, and association (*satsangh*) with the pure-minded. This responsibility squarely falls on the parents and teachers in particular and the society, in general. The best time (and perhaps the only time) to implant good *samskaras* in a person is when the person is still young and his or her negative *samskaras* are not yet ready to bear their bitter fruit. Children in modern societies are constantly subjected to negative *samskaras* of violence perpetuated by radio, Internet and television, family conflicts, and lack of training on the part of parents to properly bring up their children.

Unfortunately, in modern societies more attention is given to development of the body than the mind. Even yoga, the ancient science of the body and mind control, has been reduced merely to the bodybuilding philosophy in the West. The educational institutions teach skills that enable one to make a living to maintain one's body, but no skills are generally taught to nourish one's mind. We spend money to buy soap and shampoo to clean our bodies, but very little effort is made to clean our minds. Yet it is only the mind that can accomplish – if it can – the goal of life: permanent peace and bliss.

Karma and fate

It is said that 'karma has its karma'. Long after the Law of Karma was discovered by Hindu sages and seers and immortalized it in the Vedas, European missionaries equated it to 'fate' and 'fatalism'. Hindus do not subscribe to the idea of 'fate,' which is a Western thought largely derived from the Abrahamic religions (Judaism, Christianity and Islam). The idea of fate assumes that one's life has been set by the Creator, who is separate from His Creation. Karma is not determined by the Creator or God, but by the individual's own thoughts and actions. Thus, Karma is opposite of fate and the two concepts cannot be equated.

Does the Law of Karma deny human freedom? It certainly does not. The Law of Karma does not interfere with the human will or act. It only makes the actor responsible for his actions. It identifies God with His rule of law. Does the Law of Karma diminish the power of prayer and worship for God's forgiveness? No, it does not. A just and merciful God cannot deny to any person what they have earned. The worship and prayer lessen the burden of our karma, but 'the Hindu does not look upon prayer as a sort of "Aladdin's lamp" to produce anything we want. God is not a magician stopping the sun on its course and staying the bullet on its march', writes S. Radhakrishnan (Radhakrishnan 1926: 53). God's mercy and justice find their expression in the implacable working of the Law of Karma.

Is the Law of Karma punitive in its action? Certainly not. We are the planners, creators and designers of causes whose effects are determined by the Law of Karma. We have total freedom to make choices. If we make good choices, we bring forth happiness. If we make wrong choices, we bring forth unhappiness and misery. The Law of Karma keeps an account of our actions and returns us what we deserve. For this very reason, Hindus believe that Law of Karma is the law of universal justice.

There is nothing religious about the Law of Karma, as it is simply the law of cause and effect, providing a rational explanation of events that are otherwise mistakenly associated with divine reward and eternal damnation. There is no hell or heaven associated with believing or not believing the Law of Karma. In Hinduism, the Law of Karma is viewed as a divinely sustained and revealed universal law (see Bhagavad Gita 9, 8). The Law of Karma encourages us to rely on ourselves. When we know that our present life is in part the result of our good or bad actions in the past, that we ourselves are the architects of our lives, we can then understand that we do not need to rely on others and become dependent. When we understand that we ourselves are the source of personal power and the cause of all our failures or successes, then we begin to develop self-confidence. We correct ourselves, stop sowing the seeds of bad causes and avoid getting bad effects.

Attributes of karma

Karma has two unique attributes: first, in quantity and quality it provides like-for-like (i.e. good for good, bad for bad, more for more, and less for less). Second, the fruits of one's actions are non-transferable. We enjoy the fruits of our good actions and suffer the consequences of our bad actions in this life or in a future life. This is why some people are born into rich families with significant resources for a successful happy life, while others are born in poor families and face tough times all their lives. A loving and all-merciful God cannot create such inequalities.

In the Hindu view, individuals go through the repeated cycles of birth and death, while time goes through the repeated cycles of creation, sustenance, and dissolution. The Hindu notion of time is cyclic and both time and individuals are viewed as non-unique entities. The Western notion of time is unidirectional and in the Western system both individuals and time are viewed as unique entities. Since the karmic time is cyclic, karma works through many lives. What we are suffering (or enjoying) now is at least in part due to the consequence of what we have done in the past lives. The Upanishad says 'You are what your deep desire is. As is your desire, so is your will. As is your will, so is your deed. As is your deed, so is your destiny.' (Brhadaranyaka Upanishad 4.4, 5) Because of karma, one is reborn again and again until the effects of all accumulated karma are dissipated and one reaches 'the other shore,' moksha. When the physical body is annihilated by death, the karmic seeds remain embedded in the subtle body and determine the course of future life.

Karmic consequences must be born sooner or later

One of the frequently asked questions is that if the Law of Karma is true and just, why do some people, even when they are generous for their entire lives, suffer so much? Others who are very cruel live in abundance and happiness all their lives. The answer to this question is that the cause does not become the effect always at the same time. The time it takes for a cause to become the effect is sometimes short, but sometimes very long. There are some causes whose effects appear simultaneously. For instance, when we beat a drum (cause), the sound of the drum (effect) manifests immediately. On the other hand, there are causes which produce effects after a long time. For example, seeds take long time to become plants. Good or evil actions in previous lives all have consequences, and they have to be born sooner or later. Swami Sivananda puts it very aptly:

> If you oppress a man, you will suffer oppression in this or another life and reap the fruit of the seed you have sown in this life. If you feed the poor, you will have plenty of food in this or another life. There is no power on this earth, which can stop the actions from yielding their fruits. Such is the Law of Karma.

(Sivananda 1997: 235)

Validity of the Law of Karma

We cannot prove that the 'right thing' is always the 'right thing' to do. Yet, we choose to do the right thing. We cannot prove that God exists; yet we experience tremendous intelligence in the workings of Nature. It is the same with the Law of Karma. We cannot prove the validity of the Law of Karma, yet we cannot imagine justice without the Law of Karma. Intuitively it seems only right and just that whatever we do will come back to us in one way or the other. What kind of world would we have if people were not accountable for their actions? Wouldn't there be anarchy all over? This is why Hindus view the Law of Karma as a divine law, without which cosmic justice is neither achievable, nor imaginable.

Society and the Law of Karma

The Vedic seers discovered the Law of Karma over eight thousand years ago and immortalized it in the Vedas. From this law they derived the universal virtues such as be good and do good, speak truth, be kind and compassionate, respect parents, respect teachers, do not steal, do not harm humans and other creatures (*ahimsa*), etc. If the members of a society could operate strictly in accordance with these universal virtues, there would be no need for any law other than the Law of Karma. Since all members of a society do not behave in terms of morality and understanding, it is also necessary to have the country's laws and police. However, it must be recognized that if social behaviour depends upon the underlying knowledge base and the moral imperatives of the Law of Karma, the evil would be automatically restrained and the virtuous life naturally promoted.

The Law of Karma is a constant reminder that it is never too late to mend. We commit sin because we are more often weak than vicious, observes Vivekananda. All we need to do is to reflect upon our own innate purity and divinity, and follow the laws of nature, of which the Law of Karma is the law of divine goodwill and justice.

Chapter 8

Dharma – The Hindu Code of Conduct

Hinduism provides complete freedom in worship, but lays down a strict code of practice for life in the world. In this sense, Hinduism is more a way of life than a religion, as religion is understood in the West. The followers of Hinduism are not Hindus because they accept one theology or one way of worship, they are all Hindus because they accept the Hindu way of culture and life. The theist and the atheist may both be Hindus not because of their religious outlook, but because of their ethical and spiritual outlook in life. In Hinduism, an atheist is not the one who denies God, but the one who denies *dharma*. Bhagavad Gita 6,40 says, 'The performer of good (and not the one who believes in this or that view) never gets into an evil state. There is no fall for him here or hereafter.' Thus in Hindu tradition the practice precedes the theory and Hinduism is not merely a religion, but a fellowship of all who accept *dharma* and earnestly seek for truth.

In the Rig Veda, the cosmic order of the universe is called *rita*. This cosmic order reveals itself in the form of natural laws that are applicable to every level of existence. *Rita* is the underlying cosmic principle, which regulates nature from the voyage of the planets to the motion of the subatomic particles. The Vedic people concluded that since human beings are a part of the cosmic plan, there must be a moral order in the human society corresponding to *rita* in the natural world. This moral order was given the Sanskrit name, *dharma*. It was further recognized that there is a constant conflict between the spiritual and the material or the eternal and the temporal. While striving after the ideal, people cannot afford to overlook the actual. Dharma was thus formulated to secure the material and spiritual sustenance of the individual and the society. Dharma is the product of the speculative and the practical wisdom of the ancient sages and is the path to universal peace and harmony. It is the formula for 'doing the right thing' or, in the popular terminology, 'getting the job done right.'

The word d*harma* is derived from the Sanskrit root *dhr*, meaning, 'to hold,' 'support' or 'sustain'. Thus *dharma* is what sustains (*dharayata iti dharma*). *Dharma* includes the religion, ethics, laws of the land, individual, social, and religious duties and responsibilities; the laws of being, the principles and forces which sustain a being and the path of righteousness, rules of health, hygiene and the ecosystem as well as various paths for realization of truth. Every thought, word or deed that sustains human growth and promotes harmony is a part of *dharma*. When rendered literally, *dharma* means 'fixed position.' *Dharma*, therefore, is the fixed position of both the duty and simultaneously of the right to which an individual is bound. *Dharma* holds mankind together individually, socially, politically, culturally, spiritually, and helps the person to fulfil his individual needs, duties and his obligations to the society. The concept of *dharma* is grounded in the Hindu scheme of ethical, moral and spiritual values.

Dharma means the true nature of things and beings and encompasses the universal and eternal principles. Every form of life has its *dharma*, which is the law of its being. If *moksha* is full divinity, *dharma* is divinity achievable under human conditions. In individual life, *dharma* encompasses all systems and values as mentioned above, which are necessary to maintain a harmonious relationship between individual, family, society and the universe. The *dharma* of a student is to study, the *dharma* of a man is to support his family and the society, the *dharma* of a policeman is to protect life and property, and the *dharma* of a doctor is to cure and thus protect even the life of an enemy. In short, *dharma* is 'the right thing to do' under the prevailing circumstances.

Every thing also has its *dharma*, which is the law of its being. *Dharma* of water is to quench thirst, *dharma* of fire is to give heat, the *dharma* of an electron is to revolve around the nucleus of an atom, the *dharma* of Earth is rotate around the sun, and the *dharma* of the sun is to support life on Earth. In social life, *dharma* represents just and equitable laws, which restrain evil and promote virtuous life. *Dharma* is the idea of universal justice, involving responsibility in its widest sense, to ensure growth and harmony of all that has ever come into existence. *Dharma* is also the Sanskrit word for justice. In Hindu legal literature, the word *dharma* conveys the same meaning as the words 'ethical', 'reasonable' and 'equitable' in Western legal literature.

Dharma and the individual

In the Hindu view, an individual is a part and parcel of the Mighty Whole, but not 'the measure of all things,' as is held in the West. Since individuals derive support from the cosmos, they have specific rights, but must bear their due share of the cosmic duties and responsibilities. Thus *dharma* is the 'cosmic contract' of individual duties and rights simultaneously, to which the individual is bound. *Dharma* assigns a specific place to each individual in the cosmic family of all human as well as non-human creatures. *Dharma* imposes obligations not only towards the higher Deity, but also towards the lower beings; not only towards self-preservation, but also towards the preservation of fellow creatures; not only towards family and society, but also towards animate and inanimate constituents of the cosmos.

Thus the Hindu concept of *dharma* is more profound than the Western concepts of duty and ethics. *Dharma* admits no exception and even gods cannot claim exclusion from this cosmic contract. *Dharma* is not an idea of obedience to any scripture, deity or divine being, but is, in the words of late Professor Betty Heimann:

> the idea of universal justice, involving responsibility in
> its widest sense, not, however, in the guise of any
> external compulsion but as immanent necessity, so that
> all that has ever come into existence produces its
> specific reaction and effect. (Heimann 1937: 70)

Dharma and society

Hindu sages maintain that individual duties and responsibilities must take precedence over individual rights and privileges to protect the natural world and to ensure individual and social harmony. This is the major difference between the wisdom of Hindu sages and modern social thought. Modern social thought emphasizes rights and privileges over duties and responsibilities. The result is a rights-oriented society, which is primarily individualistic in character. Success in this society is measured in terms of how high your position is, how many people work for you, and how large your income is. This is the philosophy of measuring our lives in terms of property and possessions, and prestige and power. Since we evaluate ourselves in terms of individual success, there is no commitment to *dharma*, the foundation of civic virtue.

If we want to solve the problem of modern social evils such as crime, drugs and guns, we have to take a fresh look at our approach to life and the laws. We have to implement *dharma* in our social and political life to eliminate the economic disparity that has given birth to many of our social evils. We want individuals to strive hard, but we must also strive for the common good of the people. Every society must have a sense of *dharma*, i.e. what is right and wrong. The things that are right are the things that nurture the individuals, environment and promote harmony not only in one's own society, but also in the entire world. These are the virtues like truthfulness, kindness, compassion, honesty, justice, harmlessness, fairness and accountability, which are the operating parameters of Hindu *dharma*.

Chapter 9

Ethical and Moral Life in Hinduism

> Sacrifice your individual good for the family, your
> family for the good of the village, village for the good of
> the country, your country for the good of the world and
> the whole world for your pure conscience.

Rig Veda

Hindu religious life is based upon the universal outlook, which treats an individual as a permanent part of the Divine. All human beings are viewed as children of the divine. In Hindu scriptures, this cosmic outlook is expressed by the Sanskrit words *vasudhaiva kutumbakam*, meaning 'the entire universe is one family.' According to this cosmic outlook, God is our father, the Earth is our mother, the birds and animals are our pets, the sun, the moon, the stars and the galaxies are our guardians, and the universe is our home. Thus, every human being is subject to the same laws of growth and decay as all other created forms.

Moral and ethical life in Hinduism is not based on pleasing God, or seeking heaven or avoiding hell, but on the spiritual outlook in life. In the Hindu view, the purpose of life is not only happiness in this world, which can be attained by fulfilling our ambitions and aspirations. The supreme purpose of life is to seek perfection in life, which requires resistance to selfish inclinations and impulses and adherence to *dharma*, the law of right action. A right action is pure duty, not motivated by the thought of reward or punishment, but by pure spontaneous willing. From the standpoint of cosmic outlook, being good and doing good is absolute and being happy is secondary. The moral conduct of Hindus revolves around the three popular Sanskrit terms: *dana*, *daya*, and *dama*, sometimes referred to as 3-D Ethics. *Dana* means 'to give to others their due share'; *daya* means, 'to treat all God's creatures with kindness and compassion'; and *dama* means 'to control our passions so that our desires may not exceed their limits.' These three components of Hindu ethics are included in the single term *ahimsa*, which also includes the right and duty of self-defence. Thus the paramount ideal of Hindu ethics is, in the words of Betty Heimann, 'to be throughout life a useful member of the widest of all communities of the universe in all its dynamic processes.' (Heimann 1937: 76)

Based upon the cosmic outlook of life, the following are essential characteristics of Hindu religious thought, which shape individual and social conduct and lay the foundation for ethical and moral life in Hinduism:

- Every human being is potentially divine. All beings are biologically and spiritually united like drops of water in an ocean. Thus all of mankind is one family. No race, religion, country or culture is superior or inferior to others.

- Truth is one; the wise call it by various names. We should not attempt to destroy different forms of worship, claiming our own way to be the only right one. Just as rain water that falls from the sky eventually reaches the ocean, so also the worship of the Supreme Being by any name and form finds way to the Supreme.

- There are in-born genetic differences amongst human beings, displaying different IQs and aptitudes for different types of work, profession, food and even entertainment. We should not fail to recognize these in-born differences in human taste and temperament. We should not enforce one profession, one belief, or one code of conduct for all. Such enforcement of uniformity is unnatural, contrary to the Divine Law of life and hinders the progress of human beings in their march to spiritual perfection.

- We should give people freedom to think, freedom to believe, freedom to disbelieve and freedom to adopt a way of worship, which suits their temperament. After all, what is important in worship of God is sincerity of the heart, not the outer forms of worship. 'By intense devotion to God, knowledge of God is gained,' says Patanjali (Yoga Sutras Pada I, 23).

- Harmlessness (*ahimsa*) towards all creatures (or minimum harm in case of actual necessity) is the highest morality, *karma* is the highest law, love is the highest philosophy and compassion is the highest religion. We should be good, do good, and turn this world into gentle, harmonious, humane, and happy place to live for all God's creatures.

- The ten Hindu scriptural injunctions (not Commandments, but simple advice or guidelines) for all aspects of human thought and behavior, known by their Sanskrit names *yama* and *niyama*, are:

  1. *ahimsa* (non-injury), refrain from harming others by thought, word, or deed;

  2. *satya* (truthfulness), refrain from lying and betraying promises;

  3. *asteya* (non-stealing), refrain from stealing, coveting or entering into debt;

  4. *brahmacharya* (moral conduct), observe celibacy when single and faithfulness in marriage;

  5. *kshama* (forgiveness), restrain intolerance, impatience, and ill-will;

  6. *dhriti* (firmness), renounce fear, indecision, and fickleness;

  7. *daya* (compassion), conquer callous, cruel, and insensitive feelings towards others;

  8. *arjava* (honesty), renounce deception, fraud, and wrongdoing;

  9. *mitihara* (moderate eating), refrain from overeating and consuming flesh;

  10. *saucha* (purity), observe purity of body, mind and speech.

- Knowledge is the supreme purifier. Ignorance, blind dogma and superstition are the cause of human misery. We should seek knowledge, dispel wrong beliefs and be free and happy. Respect for learning, well wishing for all, protection of the weak, resistance to injustice and cruelty, and honest performance of one's duty are the prerequisites of spiritual life.

- Morality proceeds from the inner spirit of people. Our motives are as important in the performance of an action as is the action itself. When the heart is pure and free from lust and greed, whatever we do to perform our duties has the highest moral value.

- 'What you desire for yourself, you should desire for others. What you do not like others to do to you, you should not do to others.' (Mahabharata, Shantiparva, 258)

- Following are the essentials of good ethical and moral life in Hinduism (Tai-U 1,11). The teacher gives these teachings to the student who has completed the study of the scriptures. These teachings are akin to the address given to the graduating students at modern universities.

    ❖ Speak the truth.

    ❖ Practice righteousness.

    ❖ Do not ignore study of scriptures.

    ❖ Offer gifts to your teacher. ('Gifts' here mean respect and reverence. Hinduism is a knowledge-based tradition. Therefore, the teachers must always be revered and respected.)

    ❖ Do not cut off the line of descendants. (Family life is emphasized.)

    ❖ Let there be no neglect of truth.

    ❖ Let there be no neglect of duty. (In Hindu culture individual duties and responsibilities take precedence over individual rights and privileges.)

    ❖ Let there be no neglect of others. (Social service is emphasized.)

    ❖ Let there be no neglect of learning and teaching. [Constant learning and acquiring knowledge throughout one's life are emphasized.]

    ❖ Let there be no neglect of offerings to gods and ancestors. (Offerings to gods and ancestors mean service to the sick, handicapped and less fortunate.)

❖ Treat your mother like a goddess.

❖ Treat your father like a god.

❖ Treat your teacher like god. (A teacher must be given the same respect as one's parents. Hindus believe that by imparting knowledge, the teacher gives 'second birth' to the child.)

❖ Treat your guest like a god. (This is the reason for the traditional Hindu hospitality.)

❖ Perform those deeds, which are blameless, not others.

❖ Adopt only good qualities of your elders, not others.

❖ Offer a seat to your superiors and elders. (Reverence for old age is an important attribute of Hindu consciousness.)

❖ Give appropriate gifts with faith and modesty, willingly and in plenty, without any fear.

❖ If you have any doubt regarding any of your deeds or conduct, be like a person who is wise, impartial, experienced, gentle and law-abiding.

❖ With regard to those who are accused of wrong-doing, deal with them like a wise person, who is impartial, experienced, law-abiding, not harsh, and not influenced by others.

❖ This is the advice. This is the teaching. This is the important instruction of the Upanishads. Live your life in the manner stated. Understand it. Meditate on it. Follow it till the last.

Chapter 10

The Principal Doctrines of Hinduism

Although numerous sages and saints of all times have contributed to the core of Hindu religion, Hinduism is not a tradition of persons. It is a tradition of principles. Hinduism honours saints, sages, prophets, and pontiffs of all religions, but does not confer the monopoly of spiritual truth or moral virtue to any particular religion, person or prophet. Hinduism teaches that we must discover the spiritual truth ourselves. Hindu sages maintain that a truth discovered by someone else, other than the seeker, cannot become one's own truth unless we discover it ourselves. Scriptures and spiritual teachers (gurus) can help the seeker in search for truth, but the truth of which the Hindu scriptures speak of cannot become a truth for the seeker, unless it comes alive in their own consciousness and transforms their own life.

Hinduism teaches that the way to God-discovery is through self-discovery and not through any particular saviour, book or belief system. God dwells in the hearts of all creatures, says the Upanishad (Sve-U 4,17). As the seeker proceeds on his inner voyage, they advance from darkness (ignorance) to light (knowledge) and death to immortality. Hindu scriptures declare that *atman* (the individual self) becomes *parmatman* (universal self) through self-discovery. In this process of self-transcendence, one's own little world becomes divinised and one begins to see God in every human being, in every creature and everywhere in the universe. The Upanishad says, 'This atman is the same in the ant, the same in the elephant, the same in these three worlds... the same in the whole universe.' (Brh-U 1.3,22) This is the motto of Hinduism.

Hindu tradition is a reflection of the spiritual consciousness that is dormant in every human being. Hindu scriptures teach that through self-exploration, self-purification, and self-transcendence, people are destined to attain spiritual perfection. Hindu religious faith has its roots in experience and not in blind faith, dogma or mechanical adherence to religious authority. Hindu religious experience is an insight into the nature and experience of reality. Just as the senses perceive the physical phenomena, the individual self perceives the spiritual phenomena by a specific attitude of the self to itself. In addition to *karma* (*see* Chapter 7) and *dharma* (*see* Chapter 8), the religious life of a Hindu is characterized by the following principal doctrines.

Freedom of thought

Hinduism provides complete freedom of thought in religious matters and allows the authority of the living masters to provide correction, as needed, to suit new conditions for evolution over time without compromising its core doctrines. Hinduism considers the religious testimony of the present age on a par with the religious testimony of the past ages. It allows sharing of spiritual wisdom while maintaining a distinct character of its unbroken tradition. 'May noble thoughts come from all sides,' is the dictum of Hindu scripture (RV 1.89,1). 'However valuable the testimony of the past ages may be, it cannot deprive the present age of its right to inquire and sift the evidence' writes Dr Radhakrishnan (Radhakrishnan 1926: 15).

Because of the freedom of religious thought, Hinduism has absorbed the customs and ideas of people of different races and cultures who have been pouring into India since the dawn of history. The flexibility to rejuvenate itself with fresh ideas and adjust to the new environment is the main reason why Hinduism has survived the onslaughts of many proselytizing creeds, backed by enormous economic and political power, who bruised and abused Hinduism in one way or the other during the long course of its history.

Ahimsa

One of Hindu religion's greatest gifts to mankind is the doctrine of *ahimsa* (non-violence and non-injury). 'Non-violence in word, thought and deed is considered the highest morality in Hinduism. Without the true spirit of non-violence towards all forms of life, there can be no peace and happiness in the world', said Mahatma Gandhi (Attenborough 1982). For universal harmony, individual and social actions of the people and the economic and political actions of nations must be based upon the attitude of non-violence.

The Hindu view of *ahimsa* is different from that of Buddhism. In Buddhism, *ahimsa* is an absolute value, a supreme end in itself. In Hinduism, *ahimsa* is only a means to protect *dharma*. Thus *ahimsa* means 'harmlessness' to a Hindu and not absolute non-violence.

Protection of *dharma* is the fundamental duty of a Hindu, but it must be accomplished through *ahimsa*, i.e. with the right attitude and will to minimize harm.

Universal outlook

A religion is universal if its appeal is not restricted to any particular segment of humanity, religious group, nation, race, class or country. All religions have some universal aspects, but all aspects of Hinduism are universal. The reason for this difference is that according to Hinduism the human species is only a part of the cosmic organization that includes unconscious and partially conscious constituents of the universe. A true spiritual experience is always rooted in the universal vision of mankind. The mystics of all religions have invariably held that beyond the apparent diversity of the physical phenomena, there exists perfect unity.

Thousands of years ago, the *rishis* discovered two basic universal principles: firstly, the spiritual oneness of all things and beings in the world and, secondly, the divine nature of human beings. The scholars tell us that Hindu sages were the first to conceive of a true infinite (*brahman*), from which nothing is excluded. Thus, from its very inception, the foundation of Hindu religion was built on the bedrock of universalism. The cosmic outlook of Hinduism transcends sectarian or group dogmas and paves a way for the coexistence of all creatures under the Vedic doctrine of *Vasudeva Kutumbakam*, meaning, 'The Universe is One Family.' This doctrine guides the humankind towards universal harmony through acceptance and tolerance.

Sacredness of the individual

The most vigorous universal hypothesis humans have ever conceived is the Upanishadic doctrine: '*aham brahmasmi*', meaning 'I am the infinite, the very infinite from which the universe proceeds.' This doctrine identifies every human being – regardless of race, religion, colour, creed, gender or geographic location – with divinity and lays the ground for world brotherhood. Every human being is potentially divine and the purpose of life is to express this divinity through work and worship, says Swami Vivekananda (Myren and Madison 1993). Hindu sages have declared that no one is superior or inferior to others. Our individual past *karmas* have created us as unique individuals. But our differences are temporal and exist only at the physical level. All differences vanish when one attains Self-knowledge through a spiritual experience, the supreme goal of Hindu religious life.

Unity within diversity

Hinduism is not a religion that is immediately obvious and understandable. Unlike other religions of the world, Hindu tradition reflects significant diversity in religious thought. The ease with which one sees so much of diversity in Hindu theology, philosophy, worship and customs is as great as the difficulty in understanding the common spirit that links the diverse expressions of Hinduism into one organic whole. The religious diversity of Hinduism is implicit in two of its doctrines known as the doctrine of spiritual competency (*adhikara*) and the doctrine of chosen deity (*ishta devta*). The former requires that religious instruction should be prescribed in accordance with one's spiritual competence and the latter requires that the devotee should choose a particular form (out of the numerous forms of the supreme being) and make it the object of love and adoration during meditation, prayer and worship. These two doctrines have contributed to the mixture of Hindu religious tradition with bewildering variety of sects and sub-sects with their own customs and manners, symbols and forms of worship. There are many schools of philosophy and theology with their different religious texts and scriptures and their commentaries, and commentaries on commentaries. In spite of this mind-boggling religious diversity, there is underlying unity in the religious life of Hindus. This unity in diversity of Hinduism is analogous to the unity in diversity of nature and is characterized by five elements of Hindu religious tradition: common scriptures, common deities, common spiritual ideals, common fundamental beliefs, and common practices.

Harmony of religions

Another gift of Hindus to humanity is the attitude of religious harmony. Using the words of Swami Vivekananda, 'If one religion is true, then by the same logic all other religions are also true. This is authenticated by the fact that holiness, purity and charity are not the exclusive possessions of any church in the world and that every system has produced men and women of the most exalted character.' (Vivekananda 1991) Hindus believe that fundamental truths of all religions are the same. To illustrate, if we test five different samples of water such as seawater, rainwater, well water, lake water and river water we will find that each is contaminated with different types of impurities. However, if we boil each of these contaminated samples and condense the vapour, we will obtain pure water. It is the same with religions. Each religion has its strengths and weaknesses. If we concentrate on the strengths of a religion, we will find that each religion represents a path towards spiritual perfection.

Hindu sages recognized this truth thousands of years ago and immortalized it in the Rig Veda: 'Truth is one, paths are many.' (RV 1.164, 46) Hindu sages declare, 'As the different streams having their sources in different places all mingle their waters in the sea, so, O Lord, the different paths which men take through their tendencies, various though they appear, crooked or straight, all lead to Thee.' Paramahamsa Sri Ramakrishna says:

> As one can ascend to the top of a house by means of a ladder or a bamboo or a staircase or a rope, so diverse also are the ways and means to approach God, and every religion in the world shows one of these ways. As the same sugar is made into various figures of birds and beasts, so one sweet Divine Mother is worshipped in various climes and ages under various names and forms. Different creeds are but different paths to reach Almighty.

(Nikhilananda 1977)

Hindus believe that blind faith and dogma are the two most vicious sources of conflict in the world; only reasoned faith can ensure spiritual growth and universal harmony.

The ideal of sacrifice (*yajna*)

As described in Chapter 1, the ancient people, known as the Vedic people, lived in the north-western region of India on the banks of the rivers Saraswati and Sindh. They were lovers of nature and derived their philosophy from the workings of nature. When they observed the blossoming of plants and trees, the regular cycle of the seasons, the sunrise and the sunset, and the cycle of life and death of all living beings, they concluded that there is cosmic intelligence, which reveals itself in the form of natural laws that are applicable to every level of existence.

The ancient people also observed that *yajna* – the principle of sacrifice, i.e. one thing giving rise to another – is the natural principle that maintains balance in the universe. For example, the sun sacrifices itself to give heat and light, the water sacrifices to make clouds, clouds to make rains, rains to produce grains, and the grains to feed humans and the other creatures. The humans must in turn assume responsibility (i.e. perform *yajna*) to protect the environment and maintain *dharma* (just order) in their society. This gave rise to the idea that individual duties and responsibilities must take precedence over the rights and privileges in a society. This thought further led to the Hindu paradigms of 'three debts, four stages and four ends' of human life, which together form the Hindu action plan for just and equitable individual and social life.

Three debts

The 'three debts' are akin to three mortgages on one's life. These debts are not literal, in the sense of a liability that we are born with and spends our lives trying to remunerate. Instead, the concept of three debts reflects awareness of our duties and responsibilities.

The first debt is to God, which can be paid by worship, prayers, respect for religious feelings of all the people, reverence for all forms of life, protection of environment, and harmlessness to all creatures.

The second debt is to the society, which demands fulfillment of one's duties and responsibilities as member of the family, community, society, nation, and the world. Tirukural 214 says, 'He who understands his duty to society truly lives. All others shall be counted among the dead.' An important element of the individual duty is adherence to the moral, ethical, and positive law.

The third debt is to one's parents, teachers, and ancestors, and includes raising children in accordance with *dharma*.

Four stages of life (*varna-ashrama-dharma*)

To enable each of us to discharge our duties and responsibilities in life, the ancient sages organized human life into four *ashrams* (stages): *brahmacharya ashram* (studentship stage), *grhastha ashram* (householder stage), *sannyasa ashram* (retirement stage) and *vanaprastha ashram* (renunciation stage).

The overriding idea of the *ashram* life is to be a useful member of the family and society throughout life and simultaneously attain a blessed state in which one is content and at peace with oneself.

Based upon an average life span of 100 years in the ancient times, 25 years were allotted to each *ashram*. The three main goals of the studentship stage of life are to acquire knowledge (both secular and sacred), build character, and learn to shoulder responsibilities that will fall upon the individual during their adult life. This stage begins when children enter school at an early age and continues until they have finished all schooling and are prepared to assume the responsibilities of the future.

The householder stage begins with marriage, which Hindus regard as a sacrament and not a social contract. This stage forms the foundation for support of the other two stages that follow. The importance of the householder stage is often reflected in the analogy that just as all rivers flow into the sea, all stages flow into the householder stage.

After the responsibilities of the householder stage are complete (i.e. children have reached adulthood and have assumed their responsibilities), one enters the retirement stage, also known as the ascetic or hermit stage of life. This stage is for gradually withdrawing from active life and begining to devote more time to the study of scriptures, contemplation and meditation. Such individuals, however, make themselves available to provide guidance and share experiences with the younger generation, when requested to do so.

The renunciation stage is the final stage of life when an individual mentally renounces all worldly ties, spends all of his time in yoga, meditation and contemplation and ponders over the mysteries of life.

Four ends of life

Based upon the principle of progressive evolution of individuals, ancient thinkers recognized 'four ends' of human life: *dharma* (moral law), *artha* (wealth), *kama* (worthy desires) and *moksha* (spiritual perfection). However, they declared *dharma* to be the foundation of the remaining three ends. It is believed that the cornerstone of human life is character, the moral and ethical ability of an individual to effectively respond to external conditions. Of all the losses, the loss of character was declared by Hindu sages to be the highest loss. 'Every fool may become a hero at one time or another, but the people of good character are the heroes all the time,' observes Swami Vivekananda (Myren and Madison 1933).

Universal prayers

One of the unique features of Hinduism is the universal nature of its prayers. Hindus not only pray for themselves, they also pray for all of humanity. This is one of the popular universal prayers sung by millions of Hindus everyday:

> May all mankind be happy.
> May all mankind be healthy.
> May all mankind see the divinity in everything.
> May there be no unhappiness or sorrow.

The following is another universal peace hymn from Yajur Veda that Hindus chant for the good of mankind. This hymn was invoked at the World Parliament of Religions held in Chicago in 1993 to begin their discussion of the critical issue of environment:

> May there be peace in the heavens, peace in the skies and peace on earth.
>
> May the waters be peaceful.
>
> May the grasses and herbs bring peace to all creatures, and may the plants be at peace also.
>
> May the beneficent beings bring us peace, and may the way of all creation bring peace throughout the world.
>
> May all things be peaceful, and may that peace itself bring further peace.
>
> May we also bring peace to all.
>
> (YV 36, 17)

Chapter 11

Yoga and Meditation

Yoga and meditation are a rare contribution of Hinduism to humanity. They were expounded in Hindu scriptures by ancient sages in India thousands of years ago. The Bhagavad Gita gives a universal expression to yoga and meditation for the purpose of self-realization. Yoga and meditation are not a religion, but a scientific method or a technique of training the mind to realize its hidden powers, which are normally unknown to ordinary people. According to Hindu sages, we cannot realize God as long as our minds harbour fear and restlessness and the intellect is inhabited by thoughts of selfishness. Thus the purpose of yoga is to eliminate mental fear and restlessness, caused by the stresses and strains of the worldly life, and thereby calm the mind. The purpose of meditation is to use the calm mind to attain direct experience of truth. Yoga and meditation teach the art of right living, which leads to a harmonious life here on earth and accelerates spiritual awakening.

Yoga

Yoga is derived from the Sanskrit root *yuj*, meaning 'union'. The purpose of yoga is to lead to the super-conscious state (*samadhi*) in which individual consciousness unites with cosmic consciousness. Yoga helps to realize our true nature, which transcends the temporal, i.e. matter, mind, desire and duality. Yoga is a systematic discipline, which includes techniques for mastery of the body and mind for attaining cosmic consciousness. According to the Bhagavad Gita, God revealed the science of yoga to humanity in remote antiquity and this knowledge came down to the present age through a long succession of the sages and seers of India (BG 4, 1). Yoga provides the method by which the Universal Spirit can be seen, served and loved. In this sense, yoga is the spiritualization of human life.

Hindu scriptures describe four main yogic paths for the purpose of self-realization. They are *karma yoga, bhakti yoga, jnana yoga* and *raja yoga. Karma yoga* is suitable for a person of active temperament, *bhakti yoga* for a person of devotional nature, *jnana yoga* for a person of rational disposition, and *raja yoga* for a person of scientific temperament. An individual's spiritual path is normally a combination of one or more of the above paths recommended by their guru (spiritual teacher), based upon temperament, spiritual knowledge and *adhikara* (spiritual competence).

In the West the popular notion is that yoga constitutes physical exercises or mere *asanas* (body postures). However, mere physical exercises (known as *hatha yoga*) constitute only one of the eight steps of *raja yoga* (see discussion of *raja yoga* below) and *raja yoga* itself is only one of the four major yogic disciplines in Hindu tradition. In other words, what Westerners call yoga is actually less than four percent of the real yoga.

Karma Yoga is the way of selfless service and is also called the 'way of duty'. A *karma yogi*, i.e. the practitioner of *karma yoga*, concentrates on 'action' to serve mankind without worrying about his self-interest. In other words, the action of a true *karma yogi* is motivated by the will to serve others selflessly and not by his ego or self-interest. 'Actions do not bind him who has dedicated all his actions to God according to spirit of *karma yoga*, whose doubts have been torn to shreds by wisdom, and who is self possessed', affirms the Bhagavad Gita 4, 41. When the motivation for an action does not arise from the person's ego, the person becomes merely a conduit for selfless work (i.e. God's work) and is freed from the bondage of *karma*.

Bhakti Yoga or 'way of love/devotion' involves the exercise of emotion to seek God. Devotees of this path, called *bhakti yogi,* fill their hearts with the love of the world at large and consecrate all activities through complete surrender to the divine. The power of devotion and love purifies the mind, reduces the influence of external stimuli on the ego, and burns off karmic bondage. In the beginning, devotees may love only their near and dear ones, but with constant practice the devotion, the boundary of love, grows and a devotee experiences the bliss of divine ecstasy. Bhagavad Gita 12, 7 states, 'Those who depend exclusively on Me [God], and surrender all actions to Me, worship Me, and constantly meditate on Me with single minded devotion. Those, I speedily deliver from the ocean of birth and death, their mind being fixed on Me.'

Jnana Yoga or the 'path of wisdom' deals directly with ego and involves constant discrimination between the manifested reality (the created world) and the underlying universal reality, the unmanifest. Practitioners of this path, called *jnana yogis*, renounce their egos, but not the world. This path involves the practice of non-attachment in all worldly activities. Non-attachment does not mean disinterestedness in action. It means full involvement in the action itself, but non-attachment to the fruits of the action. A devotee of this path works without being motivated by the ego related self-interest. In the beginning, a *jnana yogi* may live in solitude to avoid the external stimuli to the ego and related egoistic responses. However, once devotees becomes adepts, it does not matter where they live or whether they are a peasant or a president. When the ego is totally eradicated, one attains the highest goal of union with God, as confirmed by Sri Krishna in the Bhagavad Gita 7, 18, 'Indeed all these [devotees of various paths] are noble, but the man of wisdom [*jnana yogi*] is My [God's] very self, for such a devotee, who has his mind and intellect merged in Me, is firmly established in Me alone, the highest goal.'

Raja Yoga or the 'way of meditation' is the path whereby practitioners, called *raja yogi* or simply *yogi*, directly experience cosmic consciousness by meditating on their own consciousnesses. On this path the *yogi* ultimately realizes that the ego and the world around us are manifested (i.e. created) reality and not absolute reality, which transcends time, space and causation.

Raja yoga, also called the 'royal path' (*raja* meaning 'king'), was systematized and codified by Sage Patanjali (250 BCE–350 CE). His work, known as *Yoga Sutras of Patanjali* or *The Aphorisms on Yoga by Patanjali,* consists of 196 Sanskrit *shlokas* (verses) and is considered the authority on the science of yoga. Patanjali is not the creator of the doctrine of yoga, since yogic practices were known among Hindu ascetics and mystics long before him. However, thanks to him the science of yoga, previously hidden in the mystic tradition, became an organized system of philosophy.

The purpose of *raja yoga* is to purify the body and mind for developing perfect concentration, which leads to perfect meditation and eventually to the super-conscious state (*samadhi* or God-communion). *Raja yoga* is also called *ashtanga yoga,* meaning 'the yoga of eight limbs or steps.' The eight steps or limbs of this yogic discipline are: *yama* (restraints), *niyama* (observances), *asana* (posture or seat), *pranayama* (breath control), *pratyahara* (withdrawal from senses), *dharna* (concentration), *dhyana* (meditation), and *samadhi* (the super-conscious state, or union with God).

Asana (a suitable body posture) assists in focusing the mind inward. Regular practice of *asana* increases body endurance, will power, and resistance to bodily diseases, as well as toning muscles and nerves. *Pranayama* involves a series of breathing exercises designed to ensure smooth (long and deep) breathing. In addition to its physiological benefits, smooth breathing also helps to eliminate unwanted thoughts, thus producing a calm mind. Sages tell us that short and irregular breathing increases restlessness, resulting in more unwanted thoughts that further distracts the mind and veils the Self. Thus *pranayama* prepares the mind for subsequent meditation.

Pratyahara includes several techniques designed to free the mind from fear and restlessness. Once *pratyahara* has been established, the mind is then directed to an object of concentration (d*harna*), which may be a picture of a deity, a *mantra*, one's own breath, or a part of the body, among other things. *Dhyana* is uninterrupted concentration on the object of meditation, which eventually leads one to *samadhi*.

Other forms of yoga

There are many other forms of yoga such as *kriya yoga, kundalini yoga,* integral yoga, *purna yoga, mantra yoga, tantra yoga* and *laya yoga*, which are essentially variations of the above four major categories systemized and popularized by spiritual masters of various traditions. All these various forms of yoga are just different paths to the ultimate goal of self-realization.

Prerequisites of yoga life

The first verse of the Yoga Sutras says, 'Yoga is achieved through the subjugation of psychic nature and restraint of the mind.' Thus mind control is the essence of *yoga*. Sages tell us that mind control cannot be achieved without moral purity including self-restraint, perseverance, dispassion, truthfulness, non-violence and non-covetousness. The foundation of *yoga* is self-control and a life of moderation is indispensable for *yoga*. 'This *yoga* is neither for him who eats too much or eats too little, nor for him who sleeps too much or sleeps too little,' declares Bhagavad Gita 6,16. For success in *yoga*, one must live a life of moderation and not a life of extremes. The string of a *vina* (a musical instrument) will snap if tightened too much, and will lose the music if loosened too much. It is same with *yoga*. Just as a properly tuned *vina* brings out the best of the music, a person who is moderate in life and who has intense longing for self-knowledge becomes fit for the practice of *yoga*.

A yogic path consists of two important steps. The first step is purification of the body and mind, which qualifies one for the second step, which is advance meditation. The purification process involves restraints and observances (*yama* and *niyama*), which must be implemented in order to develop *adhikara* (spiritual competence) to successfully undertake higher practices of meditation. Just as one cannot learn to run before learning to walk, one cannot succeed in yoga without resolutely following *yama* and *niyama*.

Yogic powers (*siddhis*)

In his Yoga Sutras 2.43, 3.36 and 3.37, Patanjali states that after attaining perfection in Yoga, one develops yogic powers (*siddhis*), such as psychic healing, telepathy, thought-transference, and many other powers associated with higher hearing, touch, taste, sight and smell. In the West, these yogic powers are sometimes called miracles. Hindus have known these so-called miracles for ages. In the first century CE the physician Apollonius of Tyana (in modern day Turkey), a follower of Pythagoras, travelled to India to study the teachings of Hindu sages. While in India Apollonius was taken to an ashram and introduced to a *yogi* named Iarchas. Before Apollonius could say anything, the *yogi* greeted him by his full name, mentioned Apollonius's parents' names, the place he had lived, and some important details of his personal life, including some incidents that had occurred during his trip to India. When Apollonius asked the *yogi* how he knew all these things, the *yogi* replied, 'We know these things by knowing ourselves through *yoga*.' Later Apollonius stayed in India and undertook intensive yogic training. After he returned to Tyana, he spoke about the wisdom of the *yogis* of India calling them 'god-men' because of their profound spiritual knowledge and miraculous powers (*siddhis*). There are many *yogis* in India even today who are gifted with various *siddhis*.

The purpose of true *yoga* is not to attain *siddhis*, but to attain enlightenment. The sages caution that those who attain these *siddhis* and subsequently use them for selfish ends invariably suffer a downfall. The *yogi* who desires the highest *samadhi* must reject *siddhis* whenever they are attained. The Upanishad warns against the misuse of *siddhis*, 'The firm control of the senses is what is called *yoga*. One must then be vigilant; for *yoga* can be both beneficial and injurious.' (Kat-U 2.3, 11)

Therapeutic value of yogic exercises (*asanas*)

An *asana* is a body posture, i.e. a natural mode of sitting or standing. Theoretically, there are as many *asanas* as the number of species of living creatures in the universe. Among the numerous *asanas* discovered by the yogis, 84 have been found to be the best and among those 32 have been confirmed to be especially useful to mankind. *Asanas* can be divided into two categories, meditative *asanas* and *yogasanas*. There are four popular meditative *asanas*: *Padmasana* (lotus posture), *siddhasana* (half-lotus posture), *svastikasana* (posture of peace and success) and *sukhasana* (cross-legged). These *asanas* help to detach the mind from stresses and strains of the body and thereby produce a calming effect on the mind. *Yogis* advise that one must select an *asana* for meditation and stick with it to derive its full benefit. *Asana* should not be changed, but perfected with regular practice.

There are many *yogasanas* ranging from simple basic *asanas* to very complicated ones. Regular practice of the simple *asanas* is more than adequate to calm the mind and maintain the body healthy for the practice of meditation, which is the main goal of *yoga*. There is a major difference between *yogasanas* and physical exercises. Whereas the physical exercises develop muscles, *yogasanas* strengthen and invigorate the internal organs such as the brain, heart, lungs, liver, spleen and intestines. Physical exercises consume body energy leading to increased food requirement. *Yogasanas* on the other hand extract *prana* (subtle energy or life force) from incoming breath and supply this energy to the body leading to less food requirement. *Yogasanas* revitalize the thyroid and other endocrine glands to maintain healthy body and mind. When performed with concentration, *yogasanas* distribute *prana* throughout the body to confer spiritual benefit in the form of mental calmness and control of emotions. Thus regular practice of *asanas* establishes psychological balance, dispels nervous tension, eliminates mental stresses, removes the heart and other bodily diseases, and promotes a healthy and harmonious functioning of the heart-body-mind complex.

Meditation

'Meditation' is derived from the Sanskrit root *medha*, meaning 'wisdom'. Meditation is not a religion, but a scientific method to experience perfect physical and mental relaxation by uniting the joy of the individual self (*atman*) with the vast joy of the cosmic self (*brahman*). Meditation is a special form of concentration in which the mind is essentially liberated from restlessness and is focused on the self within. Meditation does to the mind what soap and shampoo do to the body. Contrary to popular perception, meditation is not an act that one can perform, but a phenomenon that occurs spontaneously and effortlessly when the mind is in a perfect state of non-doing. When an individual says that he or she meditates, this only means that they are using a certain technique to create a mental state in which meditation can occur spontaneously.

There are many techniques of meditation described in Hindu scriptures. These techniques may be broadly classified into three categories: *direct meditation*, *indirect meditation* and *enquiry meditation*. *Direct meditation* is uninterrupted concentration, or a current of unified thought, directed towards an object of meditation, such as a divine thought, a picture of a deity, a mantra, or any object the practitioner may use to symbolize the divine. *Indirect meditation* consists of watching one's own thoughts without becoming involved in them. Another method of indirect meditation involves observing one's own breathing. These processes eventually lead to the thoughtless state whereby meditation occurs spontaneously. In the *enquiry method* of meditation, the practitioner stills the body and mind and whenever a thought appears he enquires, 'Who am I?' This enquiry eventually leads to the thoughtless state whereby meditation occurs effortlessly.

Can one meditate without a guru (teacher)? Yes, general meditation techniques do not need specific guidance from a guru. Such techniques are intended for a happy and peaceful worldly life with steady spiritual growth. Higher meditation techniques, however, need the specific guidance from a guru. Such techniques are intended for accelerated spiritual growth.

Benefits of Meditation

- ❖ Meditation relaxes the body by removing tension from nerves and muscles. Studies have shown that one hour of deep meditation is equivalent to several hours of deep sleep, as far as relaxation of the body and mind is concerned. Thus someone who meditates regularly needs less sleep than someone who does not. Meditation decreases mental restlessness, thereby relaxing the mind. A relaxed mind is stronger and more efficient. A strong mind, in turn, provides solid moral and ethical direction to life.

❖ Meditation purifies the mind of mental pollutants such as fear, restlessness, anger, short temper, craving, lust, and envy. A pure mind is a source of peace and tranquility, as well as wisdom and joy.

❖ Meditation sharpens memory and intelligence. The energy tapped from within by meditation has been found to gradually stimulate inactive brain cells by activating the neurons, thereby bringing more awareness to an individual's consciousness.

❖ Meditation connects one with one's self (*atman*), which is the source of unlimited power and peace within. Because of *maya* (cosmic ignorance), an individual's attention is normally directed outside of himself. Meditation focuses attention inward and helps discover own's true nature, which is full of purity and divinity. The purpose of life is to seek union with God, and meditation provides both the map and the means for such a journey to the kingdom of God. Hindu sages and seers bear testimony to this fact.

Chapter 12

The Caste System

The caste system that prevailed in the ancient Hindu society is often erroneously perceived as an integral part of Hindu religious tradition. This erroneous perception arises when people mix the ancient social order (caste system) with the Hindu religious philosophy. There is no religious sanction to the practice of the hereditary caste system in Hindu scriptures. Hindu scriptures declare that an individual is essentially the *atman* (self or spirit) clothed in a physical body. *Atman* being divine and immortal (see Chapter 5), an individual is essentially divine. Thus, worldly education, social status or power cannot render an individual superior or inferior to others. Each human being, regardless of caste, colour or creed, is potentially divine, says Swami Vivekananda (Vivekananda 1991).

Why did the hereditary caste system find its way into the social structure of the ancient Hindu society? Because Hindus failed to incorporate the teachings of their scriptures into their social philosophy. When the Vedas refer to the fourfold division of society, they use the Sanskrit word *varna* meaning 'class' and not the word *jati* meaning 'caste.' The Portuguese mistakenly translated the word *varna* as 'caste' during their colonial establishment in India.

This mix-up is quite significant because the Varna System of the Vedas was intended to achieve division of labour and help society to operate efficiently. The fourfold division of the Cosmic Being in the *Purusha Sukta* of the Rig Veda (*see* Rig Veda 10.90,1-2) is the allegorical depiction of a society which requires contributions for its four areas of development: knowledge, wealth, security and service. Accordingly, the Varna System encouraged individuals to learn skills, on the basis of their natural tendencies, which would help them to evolve society efficiently. *Varna* was not conferred on an individual on the basis of their parentage (see Bhagavad Gita 4,1) but on the basis of their intrinsic nature, which depends upon the combination of individual's three *gunas* (natural qualities): *sattva* (wisdom), *rajas* (activity) and *tamas* (dullness). Thus it is the combination of the natural qualities which established the identity of an individual in the ancient Varna System.

The Varna System must have started as analogous to professional guilds, but as a result of exploitation by some priests and the socio-economic elements of the society, this system became hereditary and degenerated over the centuries. As the Varna System became increasingly rigid, it was enveloped by another social system known as the caste system. Thus, this caste system determined the social structure of ancient Hindu society. However, the hereditary caste system was never integrally connected with the inner sprit of Hindu religion.

For a proper appreciation of Hindu religious thought, with its basic principles of equality of opportunity for the common good (*loka samgraha*), and for the perfection of men and women, the Hindu *dharma* (religion) must not be confused with or infused by the social philosophy of medieval times. Even the compilers of the ancient social order, such as Manu, recognized in their writings that a time might come when their rules may become obsolete. Thus, they declared that if any rules framed by them are found to be not conducive to the welfare of the society or if such rules act against the spirit of the age, they should be unhesitatingly abrogated or modified (see Manu Smriti 4, 176). This is one of the unique features of Hinduism, which allows it to adapt itself to the changing environment.

Free from dogma, the inherent religious attitude of Hindus is to be watchful and make changes as necessary. This flexible attitude has helped Hindu society to survive the onslaughts of time and today it is the oldest surviving culture in the world. Many ancient cultures such as Roman and Greek were born, flourished for a while and ultimately disappeared, but Hindu culture has survived. This survival is not accidental, but is attributed to the basic freedom of thought and flexibility to absorb new ideas while maintaining the essentials of its faith. Unlike many other religions, Hindu dharma uses reason and logic to defend its beliefs and practices. Hindu dharma is a living organism that naturally adjusts itself to the environment.

In conclusion, the true message of Hindu religion can be summarized as follows:

❖ The word 'caste' is alien to Hindu religious thought. The word *varna* of the Vedas denotes the class (like the teacher class, the peasant class, the labour class, the business class), a classification based on an individual's natural inclinations, training, education and actions.

❖ There are Vedic hymns, which state that all the four v*arnas* sometimes existed in the same family, where the father belonged to one *varna*, while the son to another and the grandson to yet other.

❖ Each Hindu family belongs to a particular *gotra*, which is the family's lineage coming down from the ancient times from an ancient rishi (sage). Thus, all families having the same *gotra* are the descendents of the same ancient rishi. Even today, people who claim to belong to different 'castes' in India often mention the name of the same *gotra*, when they visit temples to perform religious rites and ceremonies. This means that the forefather of people who claim to belong to different castes today is the same person if they all belong to the same *gotra*. Thus hereditary caste system is not an element of Hindu religious thought.

❖ Since the hereditary caste system, as was practised in India, is not a part of the Hindu religious thought, its practice violates the basic tenets of Hindu religion.

❖ Any form of discrimination based upon race, caste, colour, creed or gender is against the inner spirit of Hindu religious thought.

Chapter 13

Life After Death

To a Hindu, birth is the process of taking on the physical body and the death is the process of giving up the physical body. Hindus maintain that everything that is created in time must also end in time and that there is no death without birth and no birth without death. Birth and death are not mutually exclusive. Hindu scriptures maintain that the *atman*, the dweller of the physical body, is immortal and cannot die. At the birth of an individual, what is born is the physical body, which the *atman* wears to live in the physical world. Therefore, what actually dies is the physical body. People cannot die. We live in the life that is undying. Although everybody dies, in reality nobody dies. Life does not end at death, but continues in another form, which is distinct from what we know as life on Earth. Death is simply separation of the *atman* from the physical body. Just as the sunset here is the sunrise elsewhere, what is death on earth is birth in another world, known as the astral world. 'The real doesn't die; the unreal never lived. Imagine a big building collapsing; some rooms are in ruins, some intact. But can you speak of the space as ruined, or intact? It is only the structure that suffered and the people who happened to live in it. Nothing happened to the space itself. Similarly, nothing happens to life when forms break down and names are wiped out. The goldsmith melts down old jewellery to make new. Once you know that death happens to the body and not to you, you just watch your body falling off like a discarded garment. The real you is timeless and beyond birth and death' says Nisargadatta (Frydman 1986).

When the physical body perishes at death, people continue to be after death what they were before death, less the physical body. Each remains the same person with all their thoughts, desires, feelings and emotions intact, but clothed in the astral body. Hindu sages tell us that the change a person experiences immediately after death is just the same as a snake does when it drops an old skin and wears a new one.

To help understand the Hindu view of the phenomena of death and what happens thereafter, here is an introduction to the terminology often used to deal with aspects of death.

Astral Body

The astral body, also known as the subtle body, is an exact counterpart of the physical body. For this reason, the astral body is sometimes called the etheric double. *Yogis* tell us that the astral body is composed of nineteen elements: intellect, ego, feeling, mind, five powers of perception (sight, hearing, smell, taste and touch), five powers of activity (procreation, excretion, speech, locomotion and exercise of manual skill), and five vital forces (that perform functions of circulation, metabolization, assimilation, crystallization and elimination. The astral body contains the moral, aesthetic, intellectual and spiritual dispositions that have been built up in the course of living a succession of earthly lives and is the vehicle of the future incarnation.

Each physical sense has its astral counterpart, which functions in the astral world just as the physical senses function in the physical world. Thus all human beings have the potential for seeing, hearing, smelling and tasting on the astral plane by means of their astral senses. Careful training through yoga and meditation, under a spiritual adept, can develop the power of astral vision. The astral scenes are perceived by yogis as clearly as are the physical scenes perceived by the physical senses.

For every physical body organ there is an astral counterpart that provides the vital force or life energy (*prana*) to every cell of that physical organ. Just as electricity provides energy to illuminate a glass bulb, the astral body provides life energy to the physical body to breathe and function. Every change or movement in the physical body is caused by the activity and change of the astral or subtle body. The physical body is the expression of the subtle body and, as such, birth, growth, decay and death of the physical body depend upon the changes in the subtle body. At death, when the *atman* encased in the astral body leaves, the physical body becomes lifeless and we say that the person has died. Hindu sages tell us that death is a bridge between the physical world and the astral world. When death comes, we leave the physical world and pass over the bridge to enter the astral world, which is a better, nobler, richer, more beautiful and more radiant world.

Silver or Astral Cord

Yogis tell us that the psychic link that connects the astral body with the physical body is called the 'silver cord'. It is said to be a tiny, thin, cobweb-like filament made of ethereal (nonmaterial) substance, resembling a thin rope of shining silk. It has a silvery appearance and no limit to its length, flexibility, or how far it can extend or stretch without rupturing. In an out-of-body experience (such as during deep meditation), an advanced yogi can consciously leave the physical body (which remains in a state of deep sleep or trance) and travel in his astral body to regions far away from his physical body, and return to the physical body if the silver cord is intact. If this cord gets accidentally broken, the physical body dies and the yogi is never able to return to the physical body. However, yogis assert that such accidents are very rare. The silver cord extends or contracts as the astral body travels away from, or towards, the sleeping physical body. At the time of death, the astral body leaves the physical body and the silver cord gets broken. When a person is declared clinically dead, but comes back to life (as reported by Dr Raymond Moody in his book *Life After Life* (2001) and also by many other researchers), the silver cord remains intact, which allows the astral body to return to the physical body.

Astral World

The astral world is the subtle invisible universe of astral matter (cosmic energy of higher vibrations in the form of light and colour) which surrounds the physical world. The astral regions occupy the same space as the physical regions, neither interfering with the other. Yogis maintain that the astral world is as real as the physical world and is more beautiful and peaceful than the physical world. Just as invisible water vapour is as real as water or ice, so the astral phenomena are as real as the world of physical senses. Physical matter is simply the lowest degree of vibrations of cosmic energy. The astral world comprises many regions (or planes) and each region is characterized by a different frequency of vibrations. The higher the vibration of a region, the more beautiful, peaceful and blissful the region is said to be. The regions of the lowest vibrations are inhabited by souls who have lived impure lives of lust, selfishness and greed on Earth. The highest regions are inhabited by souls who have lived lives of love, service and sacrifice, kindness and compassion on Earth.

In the physical world, matter is configured into shapes and forms by forces of nature and the human mind. In the astral world, the astral material is configured into shapes and forms by thought force of the astral inhabitants. The life in the astral world is not dependent on air, food or water. Everything is composed of light rays and everything happens just by the power of thought. If one needs anything, all one has to do is to think of it intensely with concentration and the desired thing will appear before you. If you want to meet someone, all you have to do is to think of the person and you will be in front of them. At death of the person on Earth, the *atman* encased in the astral body will ascend to one of the astral regions, depending upon the moral quality of life lived on Earth.

An advanced yogi can perceive the astral phenomena by an act of will while remaining in the physical body. Through careful yogic training, a person can develop the power of astral vision and learn to shift from physical to astral senses, whenever they wish to do so, without entering into a trance or any other mental state. An ordinary clairvoyant may have occasional flashes of astral phenomena, but cannot perceive the astral phenomena by an act of will.

Life on Earth

The Earthly thoughts and deeds of a person either raise or lower the spiritual potential of a person depending upon the moral quality of such thoughts and deeds. Upanishad says 'If the *buddhi* [intellect], being related to a mind that is restrained, possesses discrimination and therefore always remains pure, then the embodied soul attains that goal [spiritual perfection] from which he is not born again. If the *buddhi*, being related to a distracted mind, loses its discrimination and therefore always remains impure, then the embodied soul never attains the goal, but enters into the round of births.' (Katha Upanishad 1.3, 8–9) In mystic language, the spiritual potential is associated with the frequency of vibrations. Greater the spiritual attainment of a soul, higher is the frequency of its vibrations. Thus each soul vibrates to its own frequency depending upon the quality of life lived on Earth. The qualities of kindness, compassion, purity and prayerfulness increase the frequency of vibrations and raise the soul higher and higher on the ladder of spiritual evolution. Likewise, evil deeds decrease the frequency of vibrations and pull the soul farther and farther from divinity.

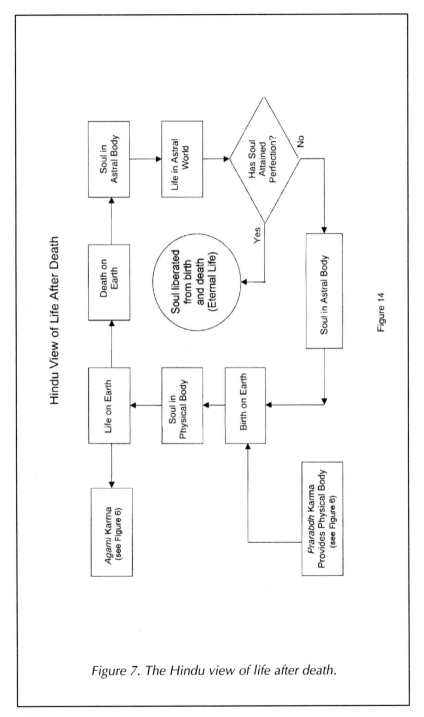

Hindu View of Life After Death

Figure 14

Figure 7. The Hindu view of life after death.

What happens after death

What happens to an individual after death is largely determined by the dominating thoughts the person has during their last moments on Earth. Sri Krishna proclaims this truth in the Bhagavad Gita, 'At the time of death, when a man leaves his body, he must depart with his consciousness absorbed in Me. Then he will be united with Me. Be certain of that. Whatever a man remembers at the last, when he is leaving the body, will be realized by him in the hereafter, because that will be what his mind has most constantly dwelt on during life.' (BG 8,6) 'It is very difficult to keep God-consciousness at the time of death when diseases torment the body, when consciousness fades away. But, for that man who has disciplined his mind all throughout his life, who has tried to fix the mind on the Lord through constant practice, the last thought will be thought of God only. It cannot come by a stray practice in a day or two, in a week or month. It is a life-long endeavour and struggle,' writes Swami Sivananda of the Divine Life Society (Sivananda 1977).

Hindu sages reveal that the dominating thoughts of an individual's life on Earth hold their attention moments before their death. Good thoughts will not dominate during the last moments unless such thoughts are deeply imprinted in consciousness during one's life. To help dwell on divine last thoughts, Hindus often chant scriptures near a dying person. The sages reveal that the sense of hearing departs last and a dying person hears what is read out to them before their last moment. Recitation of the sacred scriptures helps the dying to give up the *I-am-body-mind* idea and reminds them of their real nature, which is potentially divine.

The Hindu view of what happens after death is outlined below and summarized in Figure 7. This scenario is based upon the teachings of Hindu scriptures, supported by the authority of the direct spiritual vision of numerous Hindu sages and mystics, and is also corroborated by the near-death experiences studied and reported by many researchers including by Dr Raymond Moody.

- A few moments before death occurs, all pain ceases and the person experiences pleasant sensations.

- As the *atman* begins to depart from the physical body, the physical senses become dimmer and dimmer just as the flame of an oil-lamp diminishes when the oil gets exhausted.

- Immediately after death the individual enters into a deep restful sleep, before eventually waking up in the astral world clothed in the astral body. The individual wakes up in the part of the astral world which has the same vibration as that of the migrating soul. In other words, the virtuous souls are naturally drawn to prosperous regions (i.e. regions having higher vibrations). The selfish, cruel and malignant souls are drawn to lower and denser regions of the astral world where life is relatively uncomfortable.

- In the astral world the soul enters a spiritual clinic (purgatory) and undergoes the process of partial purification (by facing its own record of the life on Earth) before it proceeds on its onward march. The spiritual clinic provides healing to the soul and is neither punitive nor eternal. It is a temporary phase experienced only by souls needing to be cleaned and purified. In reality, the spiritual cleaning takes place in one's own consciousness wherein the soul realizes the significance of its Earthly deeds by facing its own record of the life on Earth.

- The soul lives in various regions of the astral world with the quality of life that is proportional to the quality of the deeds performed on Earth. As the soul moves to higher regions of the astral world, its unfulfilled desires of higher nature find expression in the astral world. Finally the soul sinks into an astral slumber and awakens in another world (highest region of the astral world), called the world of *devas*, before passing on to rebirth.

- In the world of *devas*, the soul's higher nature predominates. The soul remains awake on this plane for duration of time depending upon the state of its spiritual unfoldment. The duration may vary from a moment of time to many centuries. The more highly advanced the soul, the longer it abides on this plane between its Earthly incarnations. In this world of peace and bliss, the soul plans its next Earthly incarnation to work out its past *karma*.

How long is the period between incarnations? Hindu sages maintain that as a general rule, the higher the spiritual advancement of a soul, the greater is the time between its incarnations. In the case of a premature death resulting from an accident or illness, the person is likely to reincarnate sooner to finish the work suddenly interrupted by premature death. However, if a person who dies in an accident has lived a virtuous life, such a soul does not need to reincarnate immediately. In the cases where the souls are quickly reborn, memories of the previous life generally remain available during early years of childhood, after which they appear to fade in most cases.

What should be our attitude towards the dead? Sages tell us that we must not grieve for the dead, because grieving, shedding of tears, weeping and wailing over the dead greatly hinders their onward journey. Those whom we call dead are the 'minds without bodies' and they can read our minds. Thus when we grieve over the dead, they hear our thoughts and feel our pain and sorrow. They feel a sort of pull to come and meet their dear ones, but cannot do so. This causes difficulties for them to settle in their new environment. The dead have finished their work on this material plane and have further work to do on the astral plane. We must not put obstacles in their path by clinging on to them. Of course, we should send them thoughts of love and good will and remember them in our prayers. We should perform charitable acts in their name. Hindu sages teach that feeding the poor and hungry in the name of the departed ones brings great peace to them and also releases them from the material bonds.

Can death be predicted by astrology? A compass indicates direction, but does not compel one to travel in any particular direction. In the same way the stars indicate, but they do not compel. Astrology can calculate when the death is likely to occur, but not with mathematical precision. Astrology is more of an art than science.

Heaven and hell

Hindus maintain that heaven and hell are neither physical places, nor are they eternal. There is no thought of eternal hell in Hindu scriptures. According to Hindu views, love is neither an attribute, nor the quality of God. Love is God, and God is love. Love cannot bear to see anyone suffer and, therefore, Hindus believe that eternal hell is an unsound concept.

There is no hell, but there is, we may say, a purgatory (spiritual clinic), a temporary place in the astral world where souls low on the scale of spiritual development are required to remain for some time in order to be purified before they proceed forward to higher regions of the astral world. Purgatory is a sort of psychic quarantine where process of purification takes place for those souls that need such cleansing. In the spiritual clinic the soul faces its own record of life on earth. A conflict takes place between its higher and lower nature, which forces the soul to realize the significance of its misdeeds performed on earth. Sages tell us that every time an individual yields to a sinful impulse or evil desire during its life on earth, the soul is, we may say, wounded. The forced realization of its misdeeds in the spiritual clinic removes the scars of its Earthly wounds and partially cleans and purifies the soul of its mental impurities and prepares it for the onward journey.

Heaven is the name given to those regions of the astral world where intellectual desires, ordinary tendencies, tastes and aspirations, which were not manifested fully on earth, find full expression. Heaven is a place of wish-fulfilment and. since different persons have different wishes, the heaven of one person is not the heaven of another. Since creative faculties are given a free play in the astral world, the emotional life rises to higher levels. Thus a soul's consciousness rises higher until its links with the Earth and the world of matter are dissolved. In the heaven world spiritually advanced souls spend longer periods of time enjoying the fruits of their good deeds on Earth. Souls lower in development spend less time there.

Chapter 14

The Position of Women in Hinduism

> Where women are honoured, there the Gods are pleased.
>
> But where women are not honoured, no sacred rite yields rewards.
>
> Manu Smriti 3, 56

A woman has the same religious and spiritual freedom in Hinduism as a man. Like a man, she is the soul in bondage and the goal of her life is the same as that of the man, spiritual perfection or *moksha* through selfless work, meditation and yoga. Hindus have elevated women to the level of divinity. They also worship God in the form of the Divine Mother. Ancient history shows that women held top religious and social positions in the Vedic period. There are references in the Vedas and Upanishads to women sages and saints, who were greatly revered for their religious and spiritual wisdom. Today among numerous women saints of India, Amritanandamayi Ma, popularly called Amachi, has been named as one of the top three Hindu leaders of our time. However, the status of women in Hindu society has also been affected by factors other than the ideals set forth in scriptures, such as cultural customs, and the exploitation of the biological and psychological differences between men and women. Therefore, on an individual and social level, complete and total equality of women is a goal that Hindu society (and other societies of the world) is still striving for.

What is the view of Hinduism's highest scriptures (Sruti) on the position of women? Religious scholars agree that the Upanishads are the highest among Hindu scriptures. The philosophy of all the Upanishads is summarized in four verses, which are called *mahavakyas* (great utterances). These are: *aham brahmasmi* (I am the spirit, i.e. *atman*), *tat tvam asi* (thou art that), *prajnanam brahma* (*brahman* is pure consciousness) and *ayam atma brahma* (this self is *brahman*). In different ways and by different words, all these four *mahavakyas* simply confirm the truth that an individual is the *atman*

117

clothed in a physical body. Since the karmas of the individuals are different, their physical bodies are different. Thus the differences between individuals exist only at the physical level. There are no spiritual differences between man and woman. The husband and wife are the two sides of the same coin. They are two manifestations of the same *atman*. For this reason, Swami Vivekananda says, 'The husband and wife are the two wings of a bird.' If any one of its wings is inferior, weak or damaged, the bird will fail to fly.

The most important rite of the Vedic wedding ceremony is *sapatpadi* (see Chapter 15). Here the bride and groom take seven steps together around the nuptial fire (*agni*) and make seven wedding vows to each other. In the seventh vow they affirm, 'Let us remain lifelong friends, perfect halves to make a perfect whole.' The words 'perfect halves to make a perfect hole' are the final word of Hinduism on the position of women in Hinduism. Thus Hinduism provides the same religious rights and privileges, including the priesthood, to women as it does to men. The following are quotes from saints and scriptures that confirm the equality between the man and the woman in all their religious and spiritual aspects:

> 'This [body] is only one half of oneself, like one of the two halves of a split pea. One's wife is the other half.'
>
> Brhadaranyaka Upanishad 1.4,3

> 'May our prayers and worship be alike, and may our devotional offerings be one and the same.'
>
> Rig Veda Samhita 10.191,3

> 'To call woman the weaker sex is libel; it is man's injustice to woman. The wife is not the husband's bond-slave but his companion and his help-mate and an equal partner in all his joys and sorrows and as free as the husband to choose her own path.'
>
> Mahatma Gandhi (Attenborough 1982: 21)

> 'The wife and husband are like two equal halves of a soybean. One half alone will not grow. If two parts are separated and planted in the earth, still they will not grow. The bean will grow only when both parts are covered by one skin, which makes them one.'
>
> Baba Hari Dass (Dass 1997)

Chapter 15
Hindu Weddings

> Let there be faithfulness to each other until death. This may be
>
> Considered as the summary of the highest law for the husband and wife.
>
> (Manu Smriti 9, 10)

The Vedas, the treasure of ancient spiritual and cultural wisdom of India, view creation as a play of consciousness. In this divine play, cosmic consciousness, the creative source of both the physical and spiritual phenomenon, continuously evolves itself from lower to higher states of manifestation, and ultimately to its unmanifested state of eternal peace and bliss. The role of humans in this divine play is to evolve from ignorance to knowledge (*tamaso ma jyotir gamaya*) and expand the individual consciousness to embrace the cosmic consciousness. To an individual, the purpose of life is thus to realize itself, i.e. to realize one's own intrinsic nature, which is potentially divine and pure. This self-realization occurs when we free ourselves from the limitations of physical phenomena by working out our past karma in accordance with *dharma*. The purpose of Hindu weddings (*vivah*) is to create intelligent progeny to attain realization of the supreme. For this reason, Hindus view marriage as a sacrament (*samskara*).

The elaborate ceremonies and the chanting of *mantras* (sacred verses) associated with a typical Hindu wedding are performed strictly in accordance with the Vedas. To ensure individual growth and harmony in life, Vedas divide human life into four stages (see chapter 10). In this scheme of four stages of life, the householder stage, at the conclusion of the studentship stage, requires men and women to enter married life. Hindu social code allows exceptions to this functional rule in cases of those individuals who are devoted to sacred wisdom and choose to live unmarried lives. A successful householder stage will form the foundation of happiness, peace and prosperity in the remaining stages of human life.

In Hinduism, therefore, marriage is not an experiment to investigate whether or not one likes the other, but an irrevocable commitment for a lifetime relationship of one-wife-one-husband. In order to satisfy such a commitment, a couple must be ready, willing and able to subordinate their individual interests and inclinations to the larger ideal of reflecting divine love through lifelong companionship. Hindu philosophy recognizes that there are natural differences in taste and temper, and ideals and interests of the individuals. The Hindu ideal of marriage is thus to reconcile these differences to promote a harmonious life. The sanctity of Hindu marriage is reflected in the fact that manifestations of the ultimate reality take the form of wedded gods and goddesses in Hinduism.

Hindu wedding ceremony is performed in Sanskrit, the sacred language of Hinduism, and involves both elaborate rituals and colourful customs. Whereas the rituals performed to this day in a typical wedding ceremony are of Vedic origin, wedding customs have evolved over the years and vary in different parts of India. In the past, the traditional wedding ceremony lasted for several days. Today the ceremony lasts a few hours from the time the groom arrives for the ceremony to when the couple leaves for the groom's house as husband and wife. In preparation for the ceremony, several days prior to the actual wedding ceremony the families of the to-be-weds perform certain rituals at their own houses. The purpose of these rituals is to seek divine guidance for the auspicious conclusion of the wedding ceremony. The families of the to-be-weds normally celebrate a night before the wedding as a colourful social event, when friends, relatives and family members get together over a dinner, sing wedding songs and play folk dances to entertain themselves.

The wedding altar (*mandap*) is uniquely designed to symbolize divine forces, which are invoked during the ceremony through scriptural chanting by the priest. During the ceremony offerings of *samagree* – consisting of incense, crushed sandalwood, herbs, sugar, rice, ghee (clarified butter) and a few other exotic materials – are continuously made to the sacred fire, which symbolizes the divine presence. The ceremony is normally performed at the bride's home. On the day of the wedding, which is predetermined by the family astrologer based upon a favourable configuration of the stars, the bridegroom arrives to the wedding venue in a colourful procession (*vara yatra*) of dancing friends and family members. The procession traditionally features the groom wearing a head-crown, a long colourfully-embroidered white coat (*achakan*) and, in some cases, riding a white horse (see Figure 15).

A Hindu wedding procession.

On his arrival, usually the bride's mother greets the groom with garlands of flowers and an *arati* (a silver plate containing a lighted earthen oil lamp, flowers, sacred water and other materials), which symbolizes good fortune and auspiciousness. The groom is then taken to the altar, where he waits until the bride is dressed up and brought over by her parents (or elders in the family) for the ceremony to commence.

The bride arrives with a fresh flower garland (*jaymala*) in her hand. The bride and groom greet each other with their hands clasped and heads bowed in respect of each other. The bride garlands the groom first and then the groom reciprocates. The bride, groom, their parents and the priest sit down for the ceremony to begin. The priest sits facing north and to the right of the bride and groom, who sit facing east, with bride sitting to the right of the groom. The north and the east are viewed as sacred directions in Hindu tradition. After they are seated, the bride offers a cup of yoghurt mixed with honey to the groom and asks him to accept it as a symbol of the sweetness of life. The groom responds, 'I do accept' and the ceremony begins.

The priest recites Vedic mantras to praise the sweetness of Nature and the bride and groom pray: 'may our speeches be sweet unto each other.' The ceremony commences with the bride and groom taking

121

three sips of water from their right hands and then touching various limbs of their bodies to symbolically purify themselves for the sacred ceremony to be conducted in presence of the divine (symbolized by the sacred fire). The bride and the groom make offerings of incense, flowers etc. to the guru (divine in the form of guru), Sri Ganesha and other divine forces.

The next step is *kanya dana* (giving away of the daughter), performed by the bride's father, uncle or guardian. With the bride's hands filled with jewellery and/or flowers, the father places her hands, palms up, in the hands of the groom and recites Vedic mantras. The father pours out a libation of sacred water, symbolizing the offering of his daughter to the bridegroom. The groom holds the bride's hand and recites the Vedic mantras in Sanskrit:

> I take hold of your hand for good fortune, so that with me as your husband, you will live in peace for a hundred years. The solar deities give you to me for conducting family life. From this day, by law and duty, you are my wife. From this day, by law and duty, I am your husband. I declare to this assembly that I will protect you and nourish you. (RV 10, 85)

The priest now kindles the sacred fire invoking the presence of God, symbolized by the fire. As the priest recites the prayers, the bride and groom make their offerings into the fire. They both stand, facing each other as they recite the prayers for love, wisdom, harmony, progeny, and long wedded life. They walk three times around the fire clockwise reciting Vedic hymns. Walking clockwise symbolizes adherence to the divine laws of peace and harmony. A clean and beautifully decorated stone is placed at the north-east corner of the altar, where the brother of the bride is also present. The groom leads the bride to the stone where the groom places his foot upon the stone. The bride's brother symbolically assists her in planting her right foot upon the stone. Both bride and groom thus step up on the stone and offer prayer for their mutual love to be firm and steadfast like the stone. The bride leads the bridegroom as they walk around the fire in a clockwise circle three times, praying for the divine light to come into their lives. They return to their places as before, where the bride's brother awaits with a small basket of roasted grain. The brother fills her hand with the roasted grain (symbolizing peace and prosperity), which she shares with her husband. Together they make an offering of the grain into the fire for mutual harmony, long life, and life-long companionship.

A priest recites Vedic hymns at the wedding ceremony under a decorated canopy.

Now follows the most important part of the Hindu wedding ceremony, called *sapatpadi*, meaning 'seven steps', or seven wedding vows. According to Hindu law, the bridegroom and bride become husband and wife at the conclusion of *sapatpadi*. In this part of the ceremony seven small piles of coloured rice, symbolizing the seven wedding vows, are placed on one side of the altar and the bride and groom take seven steps together, making the following seven wedding vows to each other:

> With God as guide, let us take
>
> The first step to nourish each other
>
> The second step to grow together in strength
>
> The third step to preserve our wealth
>
> The fourth step to share our joys and sorrows
>
> The fifth step to care for our children

The sixth step to be together forever

The seventh step to remain lifelong friends

Perfect halves to make a perfect whole

The bride and groom now return as husband and wife to their original places at the altar. During the entire ceremony the bride was sitting or standing on the right side of the groom. Following *sapatpadi* she is now asked to sit by the left side of her husband. The bride sitting on the right signifies that before the *sapatpadi* the two were separate individuals. As she is invited to sit on the left side of the husband following the above ceremony, the two now become one – the right symbolizing the active male aspect and the left, like the human heart, symbolizing the woman as the custodian of emotion and inspiration. As the newly weds sit together, the priest sprinkles a blessing of sacred water on their heads. The groom places a little red powder on the bride's hair to symbolize that she is now a married woman. Next, the groom takes the bride out to show her the polar star in the sky. The Sanskrit word for polar star is *dhruva*, meaning 'steady star'. The groom addresses the bride thus, 'See the steady star.' She responds, 'I see the steady star.' The groom says, 'You are steady, I am steady. We shall be steady, too, with each other. I am now yours and you are mine.'

Following this part of the ceremony, the bride and groom return to the altar, where friends, relatives, family members and guests bless the couple by sprinkling flower petals on them and loudly chanting, 'May all be well! May all be happy! May all be auspicious!' This concludes the religious part of the Hindu wedding ceremony.

Chapter 16

Hindu Rites of Passage (*Samskaras*)

Hindu samskaras are described in the *gruhyasutras* (post-Vedic secondary scriptures) and are designed to promote a virtuous life by strengthening the moral virtues. Samskaras are not regarded as ends in themselves. They serve as a means to strengthen the code of conduct and develop human personality. The traditional analogy given is that of a painting. Just as a beautiful painting is created with various colours, so also the character of an individual is formed by proper performance of the samskaras. Hindu sages realized the necessity of consciously moulding the character of individuals. They utilized samskaras as one of the means to this end.

The special ceremonies associated with Hindu samskaras create a divine environment that is spiritually uplifting for all the participants. They also provide an opportunity for family members, friends and relatives to get together and rejuvenate their relationships. Samskaras direct the life of an individual so that his or her energies flow in proper channels to attain the four ends of human life: *dharma, artha, kama* and *moksha* (see Chapter 10). To Hindus, samskaras are an outward visible sign of an inward spiritual grace. They look beyond the ceremonial performances and feel something invisible, which sanctifies their whole personality. Hindu samskaras sanctify the body in order to make it a fitting instrument of the spiritual intelligence embodied in it. They provide gradual training in spiritual development and reconcile the worldly life with spirituality. In this sense, samskaras constitute a beginner's spiritual *sadhana*. For Hindus, therefore, samskaras are a living religious experience. Hindu *samskaras* cover the entire span of individual life from cradle to cremation. In ancient times a total of forty samskaras were performed, out of which the following sixteen are considered suitable for the modern age and are performed during one's lifetime.

Garbhadhan (conception)

This samskara is a religious ceremony in the form of fervent prayers for begetting progeny. Hindus believe that one's ancestral debt can be paid only in the form of a well-raised family. Begetting of children is thus considered a sacred duty binding on the husband and wife. The extinction of the family is considered to be a sin. This *samaskara* presupposes a well-established home, a normal wedding in accordance with the Vedic wedding ceremony (*vivaha samskara*), the wife's readiness to conceive, and a desire for the offspring. Based upon the medical experiences of the Vedic people, Hindu Smritis (secondary scriptures) provide instructions and lay down cautions and precautions for conception.

Punsavana (foetus protection)

This ceremony is performed from the second to the eighth month of pregnancy for protection of the foetus. Hindus believe that the power of the Vedic mantras recited during this ceremony purifies and protects the foetus. In ancient times, the pregnant woman was required to fast on this day and three or four drops of the juice of a banyan tree were inserted into her right nostril, while reciting sacred mantras during the ceremony. According to Ayurveda, insertion of a few drops of the banyan tree juice in the right nostril of the pregnant woman renders the foetus strong and healthy. This samskara emphasizes the prenatal care to be taken by the expectant mother, creates a spiritual environment at home for the would-be mother, and invokes divine qualities in the child.

Simantonnayana (satisfying the cravings of pregnancy)

This is the third of a series of the prenatal samskaras, and is performed during the fifth to eighth months of pregnancy. Intense prayers are offered to preserve physical and mental health of the expectant mother, and for the child to be healthy with sharp intellect and full-moon-like beauty. The deity worshipped and the materials used during this ceremony symbolize the desired qualities for the child. The deity invoked is Rika, the presiding deity of the full moon. Among other materials used during this ceremony are the quill of porcupine (symbolizing sharp and penetrating intellect like the sharp quill of the porcupine) and an ear of ripe unthreshed rice (symbolizing good health). Prayers such as 'May Goddess Rika make this ceremony auspicious; may She endow the child with sharp intellect' are continuously recited with great fervour. Special music, especially on the vina, is played on this occasion. Playing soft music (like that of the vina) during pregnancy is believed to provide psychological benefits for the expectant mother, promotes harmonious growth of the foetus and increases the mother's breast-feeding ability. Women sing during this ceremony to generate a spiritual environment for this occasion. According to Hindu Smritis, the wishes of the pregnant mother, especially relating to food, should be satisfied to help the foetus to remain strong and healthy. By not meeting the dietary wishes of the pregnant woman, the foetus becomes unhealthy and may either abort or deform, according to the Yajnavalkya Smriti. Other Smritis also lay down similar advice and instructions.

Jatakarma (birth)

This ceremony is performed on the tenth day after birth. Vedic mantras are recited for the intellectual well-being, long life and physical health of the mother and child. With a gold spoon the father touches the tongue of the baby with a drop or two of honey and ghee (clarified butter) while reciting the sacred mantras. Hinduism is a knowledge-based culture and considers knowledge as a supreme purifier. The verses recited during this samskara, together with the Gayatri Mantra, create a spiritual environment and invoke natural forces, which stimulate intelligence in the child. *Rishis* and *munis* have discovered that ghee and honey are conducive to mental growth. According to Susrata, a 600 BCE Hindu physician, ghee enhances physical beauty, removes hysteria, headache, epilepsy, fever and indigestion. The properties of the honey have been found to be equally favourable.

Namakarana (naming a child)

This ceremony is performed anytime from the tenth day after birth of the child to the first day of the second year. After the priest performs the preliminary rites, the mother covers the child with new cloth, wets its head with water, symbolizing purification. The priest recites Vedic mantras and asks father to feel the breath of the child, symbolizing the awakening of child's consciousness towards the ceremony. The father is now asked to whisper the child's name three times in the child's ear. The priest then announces the name to the audience and asks all present to sing the name of the child in chorus. The family selects the name for the child prior to the ceremony with the help of an astrologer. The name of the child is selected in accordance with the astronomical constellation under which the child is born. The scriptures (*gruhyasutras*) provide detailed instructions on how to select the name and which names are forbidden and why.

Niskramana (exposing a child to the outdoors)

This ceremony is performed when a baby is taken outside the house and exposed to the outdoors for the first time. After sunrise on the morning of this ceremony, the infant is bathed and dressed. Thereafter the mother takes him or her to the place of the ceremony, where the priest has set a sacred fire, and family and friends are gathered for this joyous occasion. The mother places the child in the hands of her husband, keeping the child's head in the north direction and the child's face and chest facing upwards. She sits on the left side of her husband and the samskara begins. The ceremony and the mantras used are the same as for the *jatakarma* samskara above. The child is then taken out in the sun with the mantras recited from the Vedas. After being exposed to the sun and fresh air for a little while, the child is brought back to the place of the ceremony and blessed by the elders. Afterwards the child is taken back into the house.

Annaprashana (giving a child solid food)

This is the ceremony for feeding a child with solid food for the first time. It is performed when the child is six to eight months old and its teeth have begun to appear. During this samskara prayers are offered to the deities for blessing the child with good digestive powers, good speech and mental development. The parents feed a little of the specially prepared food to the child while chanting Vedic mantras to ensure a healthy life for the child. The Smritis (Ashvalayans Gruhyasutra 1.16.1, 4, 5 and Paraskar Gruhyasutra) provide detailed instructions relating to the performance of this samskara including the type, quality, quantity and the cooking process for the solid food that the child should be fed.

Chudakarma or mundan (hair cutting)

This samskara is performed during the first or third year of a boy's age when his hair is removed by shaving. According to Hindu sages, this ceremony ensures healthy growth of new hair on the clean head of the child. This popular ceremony, often an occasion for family unions, is usually celebrated with extraordinary festivity.

A Hindu priest arranges the sacred materials in preparation for a mundan (hair cutting) ceremony.

Karnavedha (ear piercing)

This samskara is performed in the third or fifth year of age. According to Hindu sages, ear piercing prevents fluid retention and hernia type diseases. For girls, ear or nose piercing is also performed to enable them to wear jewellery later in life.

Upanayana (initiation or the sacred thread ceremony)

This samskara initiates the individual into the Hindu religious and spiritual heritage. In ancient times this samskara was performed before pupils approach their teacher to be admitted as students. The usual period of the studentship was from the twelfth to twenty-fourth year. In modern times this samskara is performed any time before marriage. In the Hindu view, the spiritual power of this samskara restores native purity (tantamount to a second birth) and, by virtue of the performance of this ceremony, the candidate is ranked as *dvija* (twice born).

Before the actual ceremony begins, a decorated canopy is set outdoors under which this samskara is performed. The priest begins the ceremony by offering prayers to Sri Ganesha and other deities.

A mundan (hair cutting) ceremony. A few strands of the baby's hair are cut for the first time during the ceremony and the rest of the hair is shaved off by a barber after the ceremony.

Oblations are made to the sacred fire and the priest recites Vedic mantras to prepare candidates for their second birth. The rites associated with this samskara carry the spiritual effect that reforms not only the candidate but also all those present. An important part of the ceremony is to invest candidates with a sacred cotton thread (consisting of three strands) to be worn around the neck and the waist for the rest of their life. The three strands symbolize the three debts (see Chapter 10) that the individual repays during his adult life. During ancient times this ceremony lasted for several days and Vedas were continuously recited by a select group of priests for eighteen to twenty-four hours. Nowadays this samskara lasts for several hours and is concluded with a specially prepared vegetarian food (lunch or dinner) served to all present as *prasada.*

Vedarambha (learning of alphabets)

This samskara is performed in the fifth year to mark the beginning of child's education when alphabets are first taught. An auspicious day is fixed for this ceremony; in India the sun must shine in the northern hemisphere. Prior to the beginning of the ritual the child is bathed, decorated, dressed in new clothes and brought to the place of the sacred fire. The priest begins the ceremony by worshipping Ganesha (remover of obstacles), Saraswati (goddess of knowledge and learning and knowledge, and the *ishta devata* (family deity). The teacher introduces the alphabets to children and makes them recite the names of the deities, which prior to the beginning of the ceremony are written on a large silver plate with saffron and other auspicious materials The child is taught to prostrate before the teacher who in turn blesses him or her. Since the guru-disciple relationship is considered the most sacred in Hinduism, even at this early stage the child is taught to love and respect the teacher. The ceremony concludes with all present blessing the child and the *prasada* of food is served to all present.

Samavartana (returning home after completing education)

In ancient times this samskara was performed at about the age of twenty-five when the student had completed studies and was now qualified for the *vivaha* samskara in order to enter the second (householder) stage of life. In those days this samskara marked end of the Brahmacharya stage (studentship), when the student was expected to return home from his guru's ashram. Nowadays this samskara is performed as a part of the marriage ceremony (*vivaha* samskara).

Vivaha (marriage)

In Hindu dharma, marriage (see Chapter 15) is a sacrament performed after completing one's education and when two persons of the opposite gender are found compatible for marriage. The marriage enables a person to enter the *grhastha ashram* (householder stage).

Vanaprastha (preparation for renunciation)

This samskara is performed at the age of fifty to celebrate the exit from the second stage of life (householder stage) and entrance into the third stage. In this third stage, the person begins to renounce worldly attachments and spend increasingly more time in spiritual activities.

Sannyasa (renunciation): This samskara is performed at the age of seventy-five to celebrate the exit from the *vanaprastha ashram* and the entrance into the *sannyasa ashram*, the fourth and last stage of life. In this final stage the person completely renounces worldly attachments and performs spiritual activities full time.

Antyeshti (cremation)

This is the final Hindu samskara, performed after a person's death by his or her descendants. In this samskara, the material elements of the physical body return to nature, and the soul (atman) is liberated from the present birth. In India, the ashes are scattered in the holy river Ganges, or any other nearby river, symbolizing the return of the material elements of the body to the nature.

Chapter 17

Hindu Festivals (*melas*)

Hindus consider festivals as a celebration of life itself. To a Hindu, every occasion from the harvesting of crops, to welcoming seasons, or observing the full moon is a reason to celebrate. Travellers to India are often amazed by the multiplicity of *melas* (festivities) that Hindus celebrate each year at local, regional and national levels. All Hindu festivals are one way or the other associated with Hindu deities, and are celebrated as an essential part of religious life. The routine life normally deadens and impedes the religious life of an individual. Festivals direct the wandering mind to remembrance of God through rites, rituals, prayer and worship performed as a part of the celebration. Such festivities relieve life of its monotonous character and make the days solemn and sacred through fulfilment of religious obligations. Festivals also provide an opportunity for people to come together more often and share in each other's joys. Such occasions sow the seeds of family values, virtue, love and devotion in the minds of the people.

The dates for celebration of Hindu festivals are determined in accordance with the Hindu lunar calendar. Although there are many festivals celebrated by Hindus, the following are their major celebrations.

Diwali

This festival is celebrated on the new moon night of Karttika (October–November). The word *Diwali* is derived from the Sanskrit word *deepavali*, meaning a row of lights. The origin of this festival is connected with a number of legends which point out the ultimate victory of virtue over evil. According to one such popular legend, Diwali celebrates the return of Sri Rama, a Hindu incarnation of God, after defeating Ravana, a demon king of the epic Ramayana. Diwali also celebrates the slaying of the demon king Narakasur by Sri Krishna, another Hindu incarnation of God. During Diwali homes and temples are lit with the glow of twinkling *diyas* (traditional earthen oil lamps), candles and electric lighting to welcome Lakshmi, Goddess of wealth and prosperity. Fancy fireworks light up the sky for hours on the night of Diwali. Multi-colored *rangoli* designs (made on the ground with rice flour), floral decorations, sumptuous food and fireworks add to the grandeur of the festival. Diwali is all about fun, frolic and festivities and is one of the most important holidays in India, similar to the celebration of Christmas in the West. It is a time to buy new clothes and gifts, decorate homes, meet family, friends and relatives, exchange gifts and enjoy fireworks and delicious food.

Holi

Holi is another very popular and colourful festival which is celebrated at the full moon in March. This festival celebrates the victory of virtue over evil and is connected with several traditional legends. Holi is perhaps one of the most ancient festivals as it is mentioned in old texts like Dashakumar Charit and Garud Puran. It signals the arrival of spring season and provides hope for a new year with new desires and aspirations. People dress in white clothes and smear *gulal* (special pink colour powder) and colour on each other for fun. Streets and parks in India are crowded with people dressed in diverse colours, looking funny and displaying erotic and occasionally curious moods and attitudes while playing Holi. People visit their friends and relatives to daub each other with colour and exchange sweets. Children enjoy spurting coloured water out of *pichkaris* (water guns). Water balloons are thrown at friends and neighbours in the spirit of fun. In India sometimes mud baths are prepared and people dunked into the mud for fun and laughter.

Mahashivaratri

Mahashivaratri, meaning 'the great night of Shiva', falls on the fourteenth day of the dark fortnight of Phalguna (February–March) and is dedicated to the worship of Shiva. The origin of this festival is attributed to several stories in Hindu mythology. On this day and the following evening the devotees sing *bhajans* (devotional songs), recite scriptures and offer worship in home shrines and temples. Some devotees observe fasting throughout the day and large crowds of people visit nearby temples and offer prayers. The prayers and worship continue late into the night, when coconut, *bilva* (Latin: *Aegle marmelos*; English: Bael) leaves, fruits and specially prepared food are offered to Shiva and his divine consort Parvati. Hindus consider offering *bilva* leaves to Shiva very auspicious. This festival is purely religious in spirit and is universally observed by all Hindus.

Vasant Panchami

This festival falls on the fifth day of the bright fortnight (the fifteen days following the new moon) during *Magha* (January–February) and is dedicated to worship of Saraswati, the deity of knowledge and learning. Celebrated at the onset of spring, this festival marks the beginning of new life when yellow mustard flowers are starting to bloom in India and nature displays her majestic best. The colour of the festival is yellow and the many women are seen in saffron coloured dresses. The celebration includes singing devotional songs, performing dances and offering flowers to the deity. The mode of worship varies slightly from region to region in India, but the focus is to pray for wisdom and understanding. This festival is especially popular among teachers and students; children hold colourful celebrations in schools.

Ugadi

Ugadi, the Telugu New Year's Day, falls on the day of the new moon in the month of Chaitra (March–April). Hindus believe that Brahma, the creator of the universe, began his wonderful work on this auspicious day of Ugadi. Therefore this day is commemorated by people reciting devotional songs and chanting scriptures in honour of this deity. In accordance with ancient tradition, astrologers make predictions for the coming year on this day. In ancient times, people used to flock to temples to listen to the narration (*panchanga sravanam*) of the new year calendar by the priests.

People buy new clothes in preparation for this festival. When the day dawns, they decorate houses with mango leaves and *rangolis* (colourful patterns made on ground with rice flour). Ritualistic worship is performed to pray for health and prosperity in the coming year. It is an old custom to hold *kavi sammelans* (poetry recitals) on this day. Ugadi is also considered to be an auspicious time to begin new ventures. The traditional cuisine includes delicious dishes, with *pachchadi* (prepared with *jaggery*, raw mangoes, *neem* flowers and raw tamarind) being the typical dish for the festival.

Ramanavmi

Ramanavmi celebrates the birth of Sri Rama, a popular incarnation of God in Hinduism. The festival falls on the ninth lunar day of the bright fortnight of Chaitra (March–April). This festival is celebrated with great sanctity and fasting; Ramanavmi is one of the five important religious fasts observed by many Hindus. On this day temples are specially decorated and among other religious activities, such as worship and prayer, religious discourses narrate the life-story of Rama as described in the epic Ramayana. One popular activity associated with this festival is the *rathayatra* (chariot procession) in which images of Rama, his wife Sita, brother Lakshmana and beloved devotee Hanuman are carried in colourful parades in major cities and towns in India.

Rakhsha Bandhan

Rakhsha means 'security' and *Bandhan* means 'relation' or 'bond'. Rakhsha Bandhan renews the bond of security between a brother and his sister. On this day a girl ties a thread (known as *rakhi*) on the wrist of her brother, who in turn gives her a gift to symbolize his acceptance of the *rakhi*. By accepting *rakhi*, the brother pledges to support and protect his sister in times of distress. A girl who does not have a brother can offer *rakhi* to any man and, if accepted, the man becomes her adopted brother for the rest of his life.

Navreh

Navreh is a special festival observed by Kashmiri Hindus to celebrate the beginning of the lunar new year of the Saptarishi Samvat, of which the current year is 5081 (corresponding to 2005 CE). This festival falls on the first day of the Chaitra Navratras (the auspicious nine days of spring). Kashmiri Hindus celebrate this day with great excitement and enthusiasm. On this propitious day, they visit local temples and bathe in the sacred spring at Vichar Nag, a town in the Kashmir valley. They also prepare a new almanac and a scroll (called *kreel pach*) on this day.

Kashmiri Hindus observe a unique custom on this occasion. The evening before the day of Navreh, the housewife decorates a *thali* (a large silver or steel plate) and fills it with threshed or unthreshed rice. She neatly arranges the new almanac (*kreel pach*), a local herb known as *wye,* dry or fresh flowers, sprouted grass, a small glass of water or milk, curds, honey, walnuts, pen, paper, a little salt, a small bread, some cooked rice, and a gold or silver coin on top of the rice. These materials symbolize auspiciousness, wealth, prosperity and all good things to be desired in life. The *thali* is then covered by another plate until the next morning, when the youngest son or daughter of the family uncovers it and then takes it first to the head of the family (as an omen of abundance), who views it with reverence. The *thali* is then shown to each member of the family as a symbol of prosperity that the

New Year will bring to the family. The family celebrates the day preparing traditional dishes and other delicacies, wearing new clothes and entertaining their friends and relatives.

Janamashtami

Janamashtami falls on eighth day of the dark fortnight (the fifteen days following the full moon) of *Bhadrapada* (August–September) and celebrates the birth of Sri Krishna, the eighth Hindu incarnation of God. Krishna was eighth child of Devaki (mother) and Vasudeva (father) and was born at midnight in Mathura (Northern India) in a prison, where the cruel and oppressive King Kamsa, an uncle of Sri Krishna, had locked up Krishna's parents. It had been prophesied that Devaki's eighth child would kill Kamsa. Therefore Kamsa had imprisoned his sister Devaki and her husband Vasudeva and killed their children as they were born. Immediately following Krishna's birth at midnight, he was smuggled out of the prison and brought up as a child of the cowherd Nanda and his wife Yashoda at Gokul, a nearby town. In his childhood, Krishna performed many miracles, but also played childish pranks, which have been immortalized in Hindu religious literature. Stories of Krishna's childhood form a part of the rich folklore of India. Krishna ultimately killed Kamsa and brought justice to the homeland.

Janamashtami is celebrated with great pomp and show and includes offering prayers, dancing and singing *bhajans* (devotional songs). Colourful plays depicting popular episodes of Krishna's childhood are staged throughout India, especially in and around his birthplace in Mathura. The activities continue until the clock strikes midnight, at which time Krishna's birth is celebrated by momentarily turning off all lights. Following this event, sweets and fruits are distributed as *prasad* (food blessed by the deity) to conclude the celebration.

Ganesh Chaturthi

This festival celebrates the birth of Ganesha (the elephant-headed Hindu deity – see Chapter 3) and lasts for a week. During this festival, devotes offer prayers, perform dances and worship Ganesha in homes and temples. On the last day clay icons of Ganesha are carried in big colourful processions for immersion into the sea, river or lake. This festival is especially popular in Maharashtra, India, where huge clay models of Ganesha are carried in a spectacular pageant accompanied by singing, praying, playing of drums and blowing of conches.

Durga Puja or Navaratra

This festival is observed for ten days in honour of the Divine Mother. In certain parts of India three days are dedicated to each of the three deities Durga (the goddess of valour), Lakshmi (the goddess of wealth) and Saraswati (the goddess of knowledge and learning). On the fifth day (called Lalita Panchami), customarily all the books within a house are collected before a sacred lamp to invoke the blessings of Saraswati. It is also the occasion for all artisans to lay down their tools before the goddess and seek her benediction upon their trade. On the eighth and ninth day of the festival, *yagnas* or *havens* (sacred fire ceremonies) are performed in a final act of farewell that marks the end of the ceremonies. The tenth day of this festival coincides with another major festival, known as Dussehra or Vijaydashmi. During the entire ceremony the Goddess is worshipped with offerings of flowers, fruit and food while devotional songs are sung in praise of the deity.

Onam

Onam is the biggest festival of the southern Indian state of Kerala and is celebrated in memory of the legendary King Mahabali, who is said to have brought tremendous prosperity to the people of his time. His spirit is believed to visit Kerala every year at the time of Onam. The festival is held at the end of August or beginning of September, depending on the position of the stars and the moon. As a part of the celebration, colourful aquatic festivals are organized along the sacred river Pampa. Thousands of people gather on the banks to witness the exciting Snake Boat races. These boats are steered by oarsmen uniquely dressed in white dhotis and turbans.

Dussehra or Vijaydashmi

Dussehra, meaning 'Tenth Day', falls on the tenth day of the bright fortnight of Asvina (September–October). This day is also known as Vijayadashmi, meaning 'Victory Tenth', because of the decisive victory of Rama over the ten-headed demon king, Ravana, which took ten days. This festival, celebrated mostly in the northern part of India, is observed with great passion, joy and happiness. The occasion marks the triumph of good over evil because of the victory of Rama over Ravana. Elegantly decorated parades and processions, depicting various episodes of Rama's life, are held in major cities and towns in northern India. On the tenth day, Vijayadasami Day, colossal effigies of ten-headed Ravana, his brother Kumbhkarna and son Meghnad are set ablaze with a bursting of fire-crackers. The result is a deafening blast, enhanced by the shouts of merriment and triumph from the spectators.

Pongal

Agriculture is the major occupation in rural India, so many of the festivals are also related to the agrarian life of the people. Such festivals are celebrated with different names and rituals in different parts of India. Pongal is one of these popular festivals celebrated in Tamil Nadu (southern India) to mark the harvesting of the crops. This festival is celebrated in the middle of January to thank God, Mother Earth and cattle for the wonderful harvest. The occasion is marked with joyous celebrations and rituals. During this festival, people decorate houses and buy new clothes. *Kolams* (patterns made out of coloured rice flour) are made in the front yards of houses to mark the festivities.

Rath Yatra

Ratha means 'chariot' and *yatra* means 'procession'. Ratha Yatra is held in honour of Jagannath, another name for the Lord of the Universe, and is a procession of chariots held in June or July every year in Puri, Orissa, India. Puri, one of the holiest pilgrimages in India, is the location of famous Jagannath temple. The main event of this festival is a procession of the three huge wooden chariots, carrying large statues of deities, each about 45 feet high with wheels approximately 7 feet in diameter. Devotees from all over India come to pull the chariots in procession through the city to the accompaniment of hundreds of priests, holy men and women, and thousands of devotees chanting scriptures and sacred names of God and creating a spiritual environment of zest and joy.

Amarnath Yatra

The famous Amarnath Cave (in the mountains of Kashmir in India) is the site of a popular annual festival on the full moon day (*purnima*) of the month of Sravana (July–August). The cave is located about 13,000 feet above sea level and has two holes in the ceiling from which water trickles down to form an ice *lingam* (pillar), the symbol of Amarnath, another name of Shiva. The shape of the *lingam* changes with the waxing and waning of the moon and remains naturally symmetrical, as if hand carved in place. The cave is considered a sacred place where Shiva is said to have revealed the secrets of the universe to his divine consort, Parvati. Thousands of devotees all over India travel to visit the cave, with some travelling by foot for months to attend the pilgrimage.

During Kumbha Mela pilgrims from all over the world immerse in the River Ganges, one of the holiest places of pilgrimage in India. This is an act of symbolic purification of the body and mind. Copyright Tony Thory.

Kumbha Mela

Kumbha Mela is the world's largest congregation of the people (comprising *sadhus*, saints, holy men and women and the devotees of God) who gather at one place to participate in the festivities of this auspicious event. In January 2001, seventy million people gathered for the Kumbha Mela at Prayag, the confluence of river Ganges and river Yamuna in India.

The Kumbha Mela is held every twelve years and is one of the most sacred religious events in India. According to a popular legend, the nectar of immortality got spilt over after the pitcher (*kumbha*) containing the nectar broke when gods and demons were battling each other for its possession. Drops of the nectar fell at four places in India: Prayag, Haridwar, Ujjain and Nasik. Thus Kumbha Mela is celebrated at these four locations. Attracted by their curiosity about the exotic traditions and the religious mysticism of India, people from all over the world travel to participate in this momentous occasion. Devotees and the holy men and women gather on the banks of the Ganges River on this propitious occasion to take a dip in the holy river. People in large numbers bathe at the Har ke Pauri Ghat, the banks of the river Ganges at Haridwar in India. The Kumbha Mela is held at the above four

During Kumbha Mela pilgrims also place floating offerings in the river. Copyright Tony Thory.

locations in rotation every three years. These are called Ardha Kumbha. The Purna (Great) Kumbha is held every 12 years.

Lesser festivals

In addition to the above major festivals, Hindus also celebrate the birthdays of many of their saints and sages. Hindu religious life is also filled with many other activities such as pilgrimages to numerous sacred sites in India and various special occasions for worship in temples all over India. There are daily ceremonies for lying down and waking the deities in temples. There are swinging ceremonies of deities on special days accompanied with the sprinkling of devotees with coloured water and powder. Many temples in India have temple cars, or boats in their temple tanks, on which the deities are taken on ceremonial rides.

Chapter 18

Religious Conversion

One of the unique features of Hinduism is that of never advocating its beliefs. Neither does it encourage persecution for unbelief. The words 'blasphemy' and 'infidel' do not exist in the Hindu vocabulary. Hindus believe in the unity of spirit and thus seek unity of religion not in a common creed, but in a common quest for truth. Hindus believe that every human being, every culture and every nation possess an individuality that is worthy of respect and reverence. Hindus maintain that a true knower of God strengthens the human heritage in the spirit of peace and harmony. The focus in Hinduism is spiritual experience and not religious authority, uniformity or conformity. Hindus do not believe that there is only one path to salvation or enlightenment. In the World Parliament of Religions held at Chicago in 1893, Swami Vivekananda declared:

> ... holiness, purity and charity are not the exclusive possessions of any church in the world, and that every [religious] system has produced men and women of the most exalted character. In the face of this evidence, if anybody dreams of the exclusive survival of his own religion and the destruction of others, I pity him from the bottom of my heart.' (Vivekananda 1991)

Unlike some proselytizing faiths of the world who spend enormous amounts of their wealth and energy condemning the other faiths, Hinduism treats all faiths with due respect and asserts that the ultimate reality is one, but paths are many. In the Hindu view, mass conversions by zealous missionaries are an insult to the spirit of humanity. Hinduism believes that salvation is the destiny of humans and one's spiritual life can be quickened only by good conduct, self-effort, sincerity and with the help of a self-realized teacher (guru). 'It is an undeniable fact that no philosophy outside India makes such a varied and manifold use of instruction in order to visualize the Supreme truth,' writes Professor Betty Heimann. (Heimann 1964: 70)

Hindus believe that blind faith, dogma or mechanical adherence to religious authority are not the path that leads to enlightenment. Hindus do not believe in using force to bring about mechanical uniformity of religious beliefs and practices. Hinduism neither recognizes any statutory methods of salvation, nor does it limit salvation to any particular person, path or prophet. If every human being of every colour and creed in every land is the child of God, it is wrong to assume that He has chosen only one religion or one saviour which all should follow or suffer in eternal hell, writes Dr Radhakrishnan (Radhakrishnan 1926). Hindu sages maintain that it is not the creed but the conduct that matters most. 'By their fruits ye shall know them and not by their beliefs,' says the Bible (Matthew 7.20). In the words of Dr Radhakrishnan:

> Look at the great saying of Jesus: 'Other sheep I have which are not of this fold.' Jesus was born a Jew and died a Jew. He did not tell the Jewish people among whom he found himself, 'It is wicked to be Jews. Become Christians.' He did his best to rid the Jewish religion of its impurities.

> (Radhakrishnan 1926: 37)

Hinduism encourages development of one's spiritual conscience and sensibility to truth and provides help and guidance to achieve this goal.

Hindus consider religious conversions disgusting and disruptive, especially those by zealous evangelists which utilizing brainwashing and other unethical methods of proselytization. Some religions try to lure people out of other faiths to their respective religions by means of mass conversions. Conversions here and there may be a matter of individual choice and preference; mass-conversions are neither natural, nor voluntary. In most of the cases, they are facilitated and forced, or simply coerced and forced. If the human race is to remain civilized, it must guarantee religious freedom and liberty in as much as one can follow, practice, and propagate one's faith without using illegitimate methods of conversion, such as brainwashing, exploitation of vulnerabilities, and offering money and other material gifts to allure members of other faiths to one's own faith.

> Even though we may give a theology of conversion, that can soft pedal all these issues [disruption of individuals and families], the truth is, the issue [of conversion] is controversial because it is disruptive. This has been

evident in many of the people I have interviewed over
the years, as well as people who had family members
convert...

writes Lewis Rambo, psychologist at the San Francisco Theological Seminary (Rambo 1998).

Although religious conversion is not necessary for spiritual knowledge and experience, Hindus do not oppose religious conversion by an individual for personal reasons. What Hindus reject are conversions by proselytizing creeds in the name of salvation. Such conversions are unwarranted and they cause confusion and violence.

When you convert somebody, you have to criticize his
religion, his worship, and his culture. All these things
will hurt him. How will he change religion? He has to
disown his parents, their wisdom, and their culture. You
are isolating him, uprooting him and uprooted people
are emotionally unsettled...

notes Swami Dayananda Saraswati (Jawahar 2003).

If a non-Hindu asks, 'What will I get if I convert to Hinduism?' a true Hindu would answer something like this: 'You don't need to convert to Hinduism. All you need to do is to study Hinduism, as it will help you to elevate your consciousness. By studying Hinduism, a Christian becomes a better Christian, a Jew a better Jew, a Muslim a better Muslim, and a Hindu a better Hindu.' It is un-Hindu to forcibly convert others to Hinduism. The triviality of the religious conversion in Hindu religious tradition is evident from the fact that, except for a simple purification (*shuddi*) ceremony, which is optional, there is no formal ritual of religious conversion in Hinduism. Many years ago, a youth in India approached Swami Chinmayananda (1916–93) and said, 'Swamiji: I need your help. My parents and family were converted to Christianity when I was a small boy. But now I want to return to my parent religion.' Swamiji asked him with a smile, 'How did the conversion take place?' The youth replied, 'We were all taken to the Church and the Father there baptized us.' Swamiji asked again, 'How did he baptize?' The young man replied, 'He took some water and sprinkled it on us and said that we were baptized.' In a jovial mood, the Swami further enquired, 'Where did the water fall when he sprinkled it on you?' The youth replied, 'It fell on my head, shoulders and arms.' Swamiji at once removed his ochre towel hanging on his shoulders, gave it to the youth and said, 'Wipe your head, shoulders and arms with this towel. You are now back into Hinduism.'

The urge to convert people from one faith to another is propelled by the illusion of dualism. The bigotry and intolerance reinforced by this illusion prevents us recognizing that the ultimate reality is beyond description and cannot be limited by the descriptions of any one faith. Since revelations were received and interpreted by human recipients, written down a long time after they were received (hundreds of years, in some cases) and translated (in some cases retranslated) in human languages by mortals, it follows that immortal revelations in mortal languages are impossible. Thus each religion or faith represents truth partially. Hindu spiritual tradition rejects the true-false dichotomy in religion and asserts that while there is only one supreme being, it has expressed itself through external nature, through one's inner spirit, and through the moral sense enshrined in one's heart. The idea of only one revelation is thus invalid. 'Truth is one, the wise call it by various names,' declares the Rig Veda (RV 1.164, 46). Other saints and seers in different words and at different times unanimously echo the same message. 'Many are the names of God and infinite the forms that lead us to know Him,' says Sri Ramakrishna (Nikhilananda 1977).

From the viewpoint of the Bhagavad Gita, numerous incarnations (*avatars*) have appeared in all religions since the beginning of time. Many more will appear at different times and at different places in future to fulfil their mission, which is to rid the world of evil.

Hindus believe that the practice of religious conversion by force or coercion is a religious perversion. Speaking at the Unitarian Church in Detroit in February of 1894, Swami Vivekananda told his audience:

> Associations, surroundings and education were responsible for the great number of religions, and how foolish it was for an exponent of one religion to declare that another man's belief was wrong. It was as reasonable as a man from Asia coming to America and after viewing the course of the Mississippi to say to it, 'You are running entirely wrong. You will have to go back to the starting place and commence it all over again.' (Vivekananda 1963)

'A truly religious man should think that other religions also are paths leading to the truth. We should maintain an attitude of respect for all religions,' advises Sri Ramakrishna (Nikhilananda 1977). 'All faiths constitutive a revelation of Truth, but all are imperfect and liable to error,' writes Mahatma Gandhi (Attenborough 1982*)*.

Hindus believe that God is omnipresent, which means that God is in the temple, church, mosque, synagogue and everywhere else. Hindus do not believe that men are born sinners and they are to be baptized or converted to a particular religion to enable them to attain salvation. Hindus believe that every soul is potentially divine and eternally pure. However, while encased in the body-mind-intellect complex and living in the world, an individual commits wrong acts born out of ignorance. Therefore, it is imperative to purify the self through spiritual knowledge, religious rites and spiritual *sadhana*, which is akin to washing off the dirt on the body with a piece of soap. Knowledge is the supreme purifier, declares the Bhagavad Gita (BG 4, 38).

The greatness of a religion does not lie in how it treats its followers, but how it treats those who are not its followers. There is no more exciting challenge for a religion than building the world of universal brotherhood, where political, social, and religious institutions and their leaders strive tirelessly to accept the people of all races, colours, and creeds and respect their faiths and beliefs; where all forms of life are revered as different expressions of the supreme lord; where harmlessness to all creatures is the highest culture, service to the poor is the highest worship, compassion is the highest religion, and truth is the highest law.

Chapter 19

Hindu Spirituality

> This Atman [the vital essence in man] is the same in the ant, the same in the gnat, the same in the elephant, the same in the three worlds... the same in the entire universe.
>
> Brhadaranyaka Upanishad 1.3, 22

Since man acquired thinking, he has been in search of higher truth. He has developed physical sciences to know the physical world, but these sciences do not reveal his inner self. The science, which deals with the nature of true self is called spiritual science or spirituality. Religion and spirituality are not the same. Religion may teach us ethics and morality and promote self-discipline, and it may introduce us to various ways of reaching something supernatural, what it often calls 'god'. Such ideas assist in reinforcing ethical and moral discipline and help maintain harmony in the society. Spirituality leads us to a totally different goal, the goal of self-realization, which transcends all mind-made rules, religious ideas and identities, rites and rituals, and dogmas and superstitions.

What is self-realization? In the West, the higher self is generally identified with body and mind. To a typical Westerner, the higher self is the individual in his best physical and mental condition. This is why the Western definition of self-realization found in a typical dictionary is 'The fulfillment by oneself of the possibility of one's character or personality.' Because of the identification of higher self with the body-mind apparatus, it is difficult and even sacrilegious for most Westerners to equate God with the higher self.

In Hinduism, the higher self (or atman) is a divine reality, man's true identity, the core of our being, and is called *sat-chit-ananda* (pure existence, pure consciousness and pure bliss) in Hindu scriptures. Thus, in Hinduism self-realization means self-awareness, a state of being aware of one's true self, which reveals our eternal being. To realize the self means to 'be the self'. This is accomplished when one silences one's mind, i.e. quiets one's thinking. Thinking is the ego activity, which generates *vrittis* (thought waves). These *vrittis* veil the real nature of the higher self, which is inherently blissful, immortal and eternal. When there is no thinking, one does not cease to exist, but is freed from ego-related thinking. Where there is no ego, there is the higher self. Since God is omnipresent awareness and higher self is omnipresent awareness, God and higher self are not different. In Hinduism thus self-realization also means God-realization.

In Hinduism, self-realization means moving the seeker's attention away from the unreal (ego) to the real (higher self) and keeping it focused in the experience of pure 'I am.' According to Ramana Maharshi:

> The body is a necessary adjunct of the ego. If the ego is dissolved, the eternal Self (atman) is revealed in all its glory. The body is the Cross, Jesus, the son of man, is the ego or *I-am-the-body* idea. When he is crucified, he is resurrected as the Glorious Self – Jesus, the Son of God.

(Venkataraman 984)

Normal human thinking has three dimensions: space, time and causation (the law of cause and effect). The human mind cannot conceive anything outside these three dimensions. It can neither conceive spacelessness or timelessness, nor can it conceive causelessness. The human mind conceives independent entities in space, succession of events in time and causes and effects of all entities, events and activities. The physical laws of nature also operate in the domain of space, time and causation. This three-dimensional thinking (or spatial thinking), however, is not valid for the description of the higher self, which transcends these dimensions. This natural limitation of human thinking has given rise to a variety of religious dogma and superstitions. Man's spatial thinking has confined omnipresence of God to somewhere in heaven, where in spite of His all-encompassing omnipresence, He is sitting there all by Himself and we are left here all by ourselves. The three-dimensional vision of things is so hard-wired in the heads of modern educated men and women, especially within the jurisdiction of the Western culture, that the process of self-realization is alien to them. This attitude also breaks down the will of even the sincere seekers after higher truth.

Hindu sages remind us again and again that the essential nature of humans is divine, but awareness of this divinity is lost when people mistakenly identify themselves with the body, mind, vital breath and the senses. Self-realization removes this false identification and bestows eternal existence, pure knowledge, and perennial bliss, which are the inherent attributes of the higher self. Self-realization is not attainment of liberation from any actual state of bondage, but is realization of the liberation that already exists. Self-realization is the freedom from the false notion of one's own true identity. It is not something that will happen in heaven after death. It is freedom from the false belief caused by identification with ego and is removed by identification of the higher self with itself here and now, in this life. It is not to follow after death. Self-realization is not cessation of personality, but is completion of personality. The sages tell us that the bliss of self-realization cannot be described in words. It is a tranquillity that nothing can shake, peace that nothing can break, and light and bliss that nothing can take from us.

The journey to self-realization or God-realization is a natural process. In the words of Swami Krishnananda:

> The movement towards God is like the movement of a baby to the condition of an adult; it is an organic growth from a lesser completion to a wider inclusive completion. Even so, God-realization is not a movement to some place. It is neither movement outside nor movement inside. When a child becomes an aged individual, it has not moved outside or inside; it is a movement in itself only, yet its dimension has increased, it has become organically more inclusive, and its awareness has become more complete. Likewise, the way to God-realization is an increase in our logical dimension, in our capacity to know, rather than doing something, running *here and there, – nothing of the kind is spirituality.*

(Krishnananda 1995)

Every human life is an expression of cosmic life, the sole life. The relationship between the individual consciousness and cosmic consciousness is defined by Paramahansa Yogananda as:

> O Eternal Fire, Thou art shooting a little soul flame of individual human consciousness through each pore in the Great Burner of Thy Universal Mind. Thou dost

appear many, limited, small, divided, in these separate soul fires, but all are projections of Thy one Infinite Flame.

(Yogananda 1975: 85)

What actually dwells in the human body is the atman. This truth is explained in an interesting metaphor in the Chandogya Upanished:

> After studying for twelve years with his teacher, Svetaketu returned home full of pride in his learning. His father, Sage Uddalaka, noticing his son's conceit addressed him, 'Savetaketu, have you attained that knowledge by which we hear the unhearable, perceive the unperceivable and know the unknowable?'
>
> 'What is that knowledge, sir?' asked Svetaketu.
>
> — 'So be it, my child. Bring a fruit of that banyan tree.'
>
> 'Here it is, sir.'
>
> — 'Break it.'
>
> 'It is broken, sir.'
>
> — 'What do you see in this fruit?'
>
> 'Seeds small like particles, sir.'
>
> — 'Break one of these, my son.'
>
> 'It is broken, sir.'
>
> — 'What do you see in it?'
>
> 'Nothing, sir.'
>
> The father said, 'My son, the subtle essence which you don't perceive, growing from this subtle essence stands the large banyan tree. That Being which is this subtle essence, in which all things and beings have their existence that is the Truth. That is the atman. My child That thou art.
>
> (Chandogya Upanishad 6.12)

Hinduism teaches that the true identity of a human being is the atman. Its reflection in the mirror of the human heart is the primal 'I' thought, also called 'ego' or 'false self'. Because of *maya* (cosmic illusion or ignorance – see Chapter 21), the ego forgets its true creative source, identifies itself with the physical body and says, 'I am this body.' 'This thought is the real Original Sin,' observes Maharshi Ramana (Vekataraman 1984). The mystery of life is that until the false self (ego) disappears from the scene, the true self will not shine forth. One of the chief reasons why self-enquiry is difficult is that it is the 'I' that has to choose a spiritual path, the same 'I' that has to meditate, the same 'I' that has to stop resisting, and the same 'I' that has to ultimately surrender itself to realize what is limitless and free. The sages tell us that the death of the ego is the birth of wisdom. It is said that 'Where I is, God is not.'

'When the mind is kept away from its preoccupations, it becomes quiet,' explains Nisargadatta Maharaj. 'If you do not disturb this quiet and stay in it, you find it is permeated with light and a love you have never known; and yet you recognize it at once as your own nature. Do not keep it [mind] busy all the time. Stop it – and just be. If you give it rest, it will settle down and recover its purity and strength. Constant thinking makes it decay.' (Frydman 1984)

The atman can be realized only through intuition, which guides one unerringly to the final goal of self-realization. 'So long as intuition has not dawned in you, you have to be guided by reason. But reason is liable to go wrong. For, when reason works, the ego-sense is present. Intuition guides you unerringly, as intuition is the voice of God. It is very hard for others to know whether, in a particular case, it is reason or intuition that is working in a person. It is a matter of inner experience for that person. Others cannot know it. But it is possible to a certain extent to find out from what the person does or says. Perfect unselfishness is a mark of the intuition… ' writes Swami Ramdas (Ramdas 1994).

In conclusion, every human being is potentially divine and eternally pure. Every human being is essentially a spiritual being that has manifested in the physical form. 'You should know you are not the body, but the divine reality (atman), pure wisdom, all-pervading light, infinite love, and everlasting joy, all put together. You are That. To realize this is to attain God-consciousness. Man, in his state of ignorance, dwells in body-consciousness. When he rises to God-consciousness, he knows he is the atman' advises Swami Ramdas (Ramdas 1994). We are here to discover our true self (Godhood). Hindu sages tell us that what we have to do is to purify our minds through a spiritual discipline and experience our true self. Spiritual perfection is our birthright and we do not need salvation, only freedom from ignorance of our true being.

151

Chapter 20

Consciousness

The difference between ordinary people and a spiritually awakened people is in their consciousness. Whereas ordinary people's consciousness is limited to only their own body, the consciousness of spiritually awakened people embraces the whole universe. Scholars, philosophers and psychologists of all cultures and traditions have studied the nature and origin of consciousness for thousands of years, yet very little is known about this mysterious phenomenon. What we do know is that consciousness is something that we all have. Without it we would not even know that we exist.

Although there are numerous definitions and concepts of consciousness in academic circles, from the perspective of spiritual life, consciousness is divided into two categories: Absolute (undifferentiated or unmanifested) and relative (differentiated or manifested). Absolute consciousness, called 'implicate order' by the noted physicist David Böhm is singular, unmanifested and the source of all that exists in the phenomenal world (Böhm's explicate order). Absolute consciousness is called by other names such as *nirguna brahman*, universal, supreme or pure consciousness, *sunya* (void or emptiness) and awareness. Differentiated or manifested consciousness energizes plant, animal and human existences; it is inextricably linked with matter as both differentiated consciousness and matter are projections and expressions of *brahman* (see Figure 4). "All this is verily *brahman*," says Mandukya Upanishad 2. The Hindu scripture Pratyabhijnahrdayam (The Doctrine of Recognition), sutra 5 reveals:

> *Citi* [absolute consciousness] itself descends from
> *cetana* [undifferentiated state] and becomes *citta*
> [differentiated consciousness] inasmuch as it becomes
> differentiated in conformity with the objects of
> consciousness [*cetya*].

The expression of the absolute consciousness (nameless and formless reality) in the phenomenal world (the reality with name and form) depends upon the physical and material configuration of the objects of consciousness. Thus consciousness associated with inanimate matter only expresses as atomic and molecular forces that hold the matter together. Manifested consciousness and matter can be compared to the two wings of a bird where the bird is the absolute undifferentiated consciousness and is the most important entity. If the bird were not there the wings would not be there. Manifested consciousness expresses as plant consciousness in plants and animal consciousness in animals. The highest manifestation of consciousness occurs in human body, wherein it illuminates the mind and makes human life possible.

Brahman manifests in the phenomenal world as spirit (consciousness) and nature (*prakriti* or matter). *Brahman* is the stage on which the spirit and nature dance together, symbolized by Shiva's dance in Hindu scriptures (see Figure 11). This eternal dance is made possible by *prakriti* (or *maya*), the inherent creative energy of *brahman*. In this eternal dance *brahman* manifests in diverse forms in the phenomenal world (creation), stays in that mode for a time (sustenance), and reverts back to the original state (dissolution). In the beginning of creation, consciousness is wrapped up in matter. Through the process of evolution, consciousness evolves from lower forms to higher forms of life until it becomes aware of itself in a human body. From that stage onwards, it struggles to free itself from physical limitations (through spiritual discipline) and attain union with *brahman*, the original source of consciousness.

According to Hindu views, consciousness connects nameless and formless reality (absolute consciousness) to the reality with name and form (physical phenomena). Consciousness is the link that gives us the power to recognize the illusory separation between the nameless and formless world (spiritual world) and the world of name and form (material world).

The individual consciousness is the result of differentiation of pure consciousness into a centre of experience in the act of creation. The subject-object polarization develops through this differentiation. Individual consciousness is not produced by the brain, nor is consciousness a quality of the brain. The brain is only a vehicle of consciousness. 'It is a part of Cartesian mode to think of consciousness as being something peculiar to the head, that the head is the organ originating consciousness. It isn't. The head is the organ that inflects consciousness in a certain direction, or to ascertain set of purposes.

But there is a consciousness here in the body. The whole living world is informed by consciousness' writes Joseph Campbell (Campbell 1988).

Consciousness is, therefore, the cause and not the effect of the brain activities. The brain itself is the object of consciousness. If you close your eyes, relax the body and mind, and focus attention on each region of the brain, you can perceive each part of the brain. According to the law of perception the subject and the object must be separate and distinct from each other for perception to take place. Is consciousness the bulb that carries the light or is it the light of which the bulb is a vehicle? The correct answer is that consciousness is the light of which the bulb (i.e. human body and brain) is a vehicle. Instead of the human beings possessing consciousness, it is the consciousness, which possesses the human beings. Ordinary human consciousness '… being a product of conditions and circumstances, depends on them and changes along with them. What is independent, uncreated, timeless and changeless, and yet ever new and fresh, is beyond the mind. When the mind thinks of it, the mind dissolves and only happiness remains' says Nisargadatta Mahraj (Frydman 1982).

In the absence of spiritual awakening, human consciousness is limited to one's body and mind apparatus alone and only perceives differences and distinctions in the physical phenomena. It is not trained to perceive the underlying unity. Consciousness tells you that you exist as a separate entity. Thus an individual believes himself or herself to be separate from God and everything else. This creates an illusion of separation, which further causes individuals to believe that everyone else is a threat to their own existence. Ordinary human consciousness is the medium of duality and cannot transcend the duality unless it is trained to evolve and expand to embrace the universal consciousness. The emerging change in consciousness is the challenge and the key. 'Our future depends on whether we feel like part of this one Whole (non-dual Brahman) or whether we feel we're separate' writes David Böhm.

Upanishads describe the three stages of consciousness that spiritual aspirants frequently experience on their spiritual path. The first stage is that of dualism where aspirants worship God or any divine being (such as Krishna, Christ or Buddha). When their devotion becomes deeper their consciousness rises to the second stage, which is the stage of qualified non-dualism. They begin to experience the divine presence which pervades everything that exists. An aspirant realizes that God is both immanent and transcendent. The famous mystic woman saint of Kashmir, Lalleshawri, describes this vision of ultimate reality as follows:

> While I wandered in search of Him. Then lo! All of a sudden, I saw that. He was all and everywhere. I had nowhere to go in search of Him. This was the Truth of a hundred truths. Whoever learns of it, will they not wonder? Will they not be mad for joy?

Another mystic of Kashmir, Nund Rishi, (1377–1442 CE) describes the same vision in different words:

> He's beside me and I'm beside Him. Blissful I feel with Him. In vain, I went seeking Him in strange lands, but My Friend Himself graced me in my own House!

Continued devotion and the spiritual practice enables the aspirant to go beyond the qualified dualistic state of consciousness to reach the state of super-consciousness, which is the final goal of spiritual life. This state of consciousness is the non-dual state of perfect unity where aspirants experience their existence and the divine existence as identical. This state is indicated in the statement of the Chandogya Upanishad '*Tat tvam asi*' meaning 'That [non-dual Brahman] thou art.' Jesus revealed the same truth, 'I and my father are one.' (John 10: 30) Swami Sivananda, a famous nineteenth-century saint of India, describes the non-dual spiritual experience as follows:

> All dualities vanish here. There is neither subject nor object. There is neither darkness nor void in this experience. It is all light. There is nothing but the Self. It is a grand experience. It is limitless, division-less, and infinite, an experience of being and of pure consciousness. You will be struck with awe and wonder.

> (Sivananda 1997: 337)

Duality is the phenomena of time and space domains. The Garden of Eden is a metaphor for the beingness, which transcends pairs of opposites, and is the absolute consciousness, which is unaware of itself, writes Swami Sivananda (Sivananda 1997). Moving out of the sphere of limited individual consciousness to the cosmic plane of consciousness, the wonder of all is the cherished goal of spiritual life. The cosmic plane is unnamable, as it transcends all names, and can be known as the Upanishad says 'The subtle Self is known by thought in which the senses in five different forms have centred. The whole of men's thought is pervaded by the senses. When thought is purified, the Self shines forth.' (Mundaka Upanishads 3.1, 9)

Chapter 21

Maya – The Illusions of Human Thinking

> Maya projects multiplicity. Maya creates division,
> division between the individual soul and the Supreme
> Soul. Just as a stick burning at one end, when waved
> round quickly, produces an illusion of a circle of fire, so
> is it with the multiplicity of the world. Maya deludes us.

(Sivananda 1997:283–8)

Maya is a popular word in Hindu religious, spiritual and philosophical literature and is used with different connotations in different contexts. 'The Sanskrit word *maya* means 'the measurer'; it is the magical power in creation by which limitations and divisions are apparently present in the Immeasurable and Inseparable. Maya is Nature herself – the phenomenal worlds, ever in transitional flux as antithesis to Divine Immutability' writes Parmahansa Yogananda (Yogananda 1992: 460). From the spiritual perspective, maya is the veiling and obscuring twin power of Nature, which creates illusion in our perception. What is meant by illusion? A person is said to be under illusion when he declares something to be other than what it really is. In other words, he takes as true or real something which is neither. The classic metaphor illustrating how maya operates is that of seeing a rope as a snake. In twilight, a person may see a coiled rope as a snake, but the snake disappears in the bright light of the sun and the rope is seen as it really is. In this example, a person seeing the rope as a snake is under illusion because he sees something (a rope) but misinterprets it as something else (a snake).

Maya helps man to attain superior worldly knowledge, but at the same time deceives him by creating a false notion of his own being. 'Under the spell of God's maya, man forgets his true nature. He forgets that he is heir to the infinite glories of his Father. Maya induces people to live like silkworms. The worms can cut through the cocoons if they want, but having woven the cocoons themselves, they are too much attached to them to leave them. And so they die there' says Paramahamsa Sri

Ramakrishna (Nikhilananda 1977). Maya creates a sense of differentiation in us. It conceals the higher reality from us in the first place and then projects it to us as something else. Maya strengthens our attachment to the material world and hampers our will to know who we really are. In this sense, maya is ignorance (*avidya*) or impurity.

'Maya is the ignorance that darkens our consciousness and tends to limit it within the boundaries of our personal self (ego). It is this *Avidya*, this ignorance, this limiting of consciousness that creates the hard separateness of ego, and thus becomes the source of all pride, greed and cruelty incidental to self-seeking... 'writes Rabindranath Tagore, Nobel laureate for literature. If maya is the cause of ignorance, then why has God created it? 'That is His play,' replies Paramahamsa Sri Ramakrishna (Nikhilananda 1997). Sri Ramakrishna explains:

> The glory of light cannot be appreciated without darkness. Happiness cannot be understood without misery. The knowledge of good is possible because of the knowledge of evil. Maya may be likened to the skin of a mango. The mango grows and ripens because of the presence of its covering skin. You throw away the skin when the mango is fully ripe and ready to be eaten. [Likewise] it is possible for a man to attain gradually to the knowledge of Brahman because of [the presence of the] covering skin of maya. It [maya] is necessary...

(Nikhilananda 1997: 216)

According to Hindu scriptures, the ultimate reality is infinite, undivided and changeless. But, under the influence of maya, we see this reality divided into finite things and beings of the world, changing in space and time. Thus maya is a mistaken way of looking at the world. It allows us to perceive the world, but differently to what it really is. Under the spell of maya, an ordinary person sees the world only as a show of fleeing names and forms. Upon attainment of self-knowledge, the person transcends maya, sees God everywhere, and ceases to see the differences created by the body-mind-ego complex. The world does not disappear for them, but presents itself as the glory of God, a divine play (*lila*). Worldly people are interested in the names and forms of the gold ornaments, but a self-realized person looks upon them only as gold through and through, observes Swami Shivananda (Sivavananda 1997).

Sages and seers remind us that because of maya our aims, objectives and interests keep changing from early childhood to old age. For a baby the mother is reality and all else is maya. For a child, toys are the reality and everything else, including his mother, is maya. For a young person, new interests in the form of work, wealth, family, art and research become the reality and everything else is maya. In old age, the earlier pursuits of one's life become trivial and desire to know the higher reality becomes the reality. In the case of a fortunate few, gifted with vision and wisdom, self-realization is the reality right from a young age, as is evident from the lives of saints and seers of all religions and cultures.

Maya is the mother of all worldly illusions. 'The Self of every man is an integral part of God... When this is the true law, why do we human beings experience imperfection, why do we feel broken and scattered, and why do we keep crying out and weeping? The reason is our forgetfulness of our own real nature. Although illusory, this Self-forgetfulness is very powerful. It has been called ignorance, nescience, *maya*, or impurity' writes Swami Muktananda (Muktananda 1978:6). Hindu saints and seers remind us that we must overcome the following four maya-created illusions in order to succeed on our journey to Self-awareness.

Illusion of separateness

The illusion of separateness induces us to believe that God has magically created us from nothing, separate from himself and from everything else in the nature. Hindu saints and seers assert that the illusion of separateness is the first major hurdle in one's spiritual path. Scriptures declare that while we perceive diversity in the nature due to maya, in reality there is oneness behind the great multiplicity of things and beings in the universe. Rig Veda declares: 'Truth is one, sages call it by various names.' (RV 1.164, 46) Sri Krishna says in the Bhagavad Gita, 'He who sees Me [the Universal Self] present in all beings existing within Me, never loses sight of Me, and I never lose sight of him.' (BG 6, 30) Sri Aurobindo writes: 'In nature, therefore, all things that exist, animate or inanimate, are becomings of the one Self of all. All these different creatures are one indivisible existence.' (Aurobindo 1985) At the World Parliament of Religions held in Chicago in 1893, Swami Vivekananda declared: 'Unity in variety is the plan of nature.' (Vivekananda 1991) The Upanishads declare: 'There is one Supreme Ruler, the inmost Self of all beings, who makes His own form manifold.

Eternal happiness belongs to the wise, who perceive Him within themselves.' (Katha Upanishad 2.2, 12)

Sages and scriptures reveal that the illusion of separateness must be overcome by recognizing that all things and beings are different manifestations of one Reality, call it what you may – *brahman*, God, consciousness, awareness, the absolute. This mental attitude, i.e. recognition of unity in diversity, is the first critical step in one's journey to self-awareness. Finally this unity is realized by the individual in every part of his being through his own spiritual experience.

Illusion of materiality

The illusion of materiality leads us to the notion that there is only material reality and physical things and objects are all that exist. This illusion leads to the erroneous view that big is better and our self-image and worth are determined by what we possess, and not by who we are. This attitude results in our attachment to the physical world and lust for material wealth.

Sages and seers of all religions emphasize that attachment to material objects is another major hurdle in one's spiritual path, since higher reality is immaterial. The Bhagavad Gita declares, 'When a man ceases to have any attachment either for the object of senses or for actions, and has renounced all thoughts of the world, he is said to have climbed to the heights of yoga.' (BG 6, 4). This does not mean that we should not acquire material wealth and satisfy our genuine needs and desires. In Hinduism wealth (*artha*) is considered as one of the four legitimate ends of human life, the other three being *dharma* (righteousness), *kama* (fulfillment of noble desires), and *moksha* (liberation or spiritual freedom). What the Bhagavad Gita teaches is that acquiring wealth should not become the single end of one's life. The sages advise that we should be like lotus that grows in mud, but is not stained by it.

Illusion of rationality

The illusion of rationality leads us to believe that all we can know is what we perceive through our senses. We tend to believe that reason is the highest tool of knowledge and will solve all life's problems. We think that reason can give us a true understanding of what we really are, the world around us, and will lead us to permanent peace and bliss. The sages and saints of all cultures remind us that reason is a limited tool and cannot reach the final truth. It helps us only to a limit and after that it becomes a hindrance. Reason cannot be a safe guide throughout the spiritual journey. 'If you want to take a leap into the Infinite and realize your oneness with It, you have to stop reasoning,' advises Swami Ramdas (Ramdas 1994).

Hindu scriptures classify knowledge into two categories: rational or lower knowledge (*para vidya*) and higher or intuitive knowledge (*apara vidya*). The lower knowledge consists of worldly knowledge such as humanities, arts and sciences, which are necessary in order to enhance our physical aspect of life. We are, however, spiritual beings with physical bodies and not vice versa. Love, freedom and peace are spiritual essence of the atman and cannot be realized through material wealth and abundance alone. Rational knowledge is inadequate to understand the aim of our lives, our relationship with human beings, other creatures, and with God. 'Thought can grasp the unfolded (physical phenomena), but only something beyond thought – intuition, unmediated insight, intelligence – can experience the enfolded (what is beyond physical phenomena)... ' says David Böhm.

Sages tell us that the intellect often works as an instrument of the ego. This is why reason often separates rather than unites. A reasonable man is not necessarily a virtuous man, because often he uses reason to fulfil his own selfish ends. Rational knowledge is based upon the process of minutely analyzing and dissecting the objects of study and magnifying the differences. Such an approach is useful when studying arts and sciences, but is totally inadequate when seeking knowledge about who we really are and our true relationship with other humans. Rational knowledge in the form of intellectual consciousness divides humanity into castes and creeds, and believers and non-believers. 'The break in the normal and natural order of things in human life is directly traceable to man's intellectuality... ' writes Dr Radhakrishnan (Radhakrishnan 1940).

The higher or intuitive knowledge is the knowledge of the whole, which can be attained only through meditation and contemplation. The intuitive process of acquiring knowledge is expressed in the Upanishads in many phrases such as 'knowing by becoming' and 'to know *brahman* is to become *brahman*.' (Brh-U 1.4, 10) The sages and saints proclaim that higher knowledge is a matter of *being* rather than *just doing* and true knowledge is synthetic and unifying and not analytic and divisive. In our endeavour to know others and ourselves truly, we should not treat others as objects, but as 'I's' and 'thou's', advise Hindu sages and seers.

Illusion of duality

The illusion of duality (or dualism) is the most powerful illusion that leads to the true-false dichotomy in ethics and religion. In ethics this illusion induces us to think that an act is only either right or wrong, or good or bad. Hindu sages adopt a monistic viewpoint, according to which truth is a matter of degree. While we must adopt the truth in all situations and circumstances, we must recognize that the truth and falsehood are usually shared. The illusion of dualism in ethics often leads us to think that our views are right and those of other's are wrong. It induces us to use evil means to attain good ends. Ends and means cannot be separated, writes Mahatma Gandhi (Attenborough 1982). Only through good means should good ends be realized.

The illusion of dualism in religion leads to the true-false dichotomies, such as believers-nonbelievers, saved-unsaved and redeemed-unredeemed. The religions that have accepted such dichotomies have historically become divisive and created hatred among people. History shows that such religions have brought more misery to mankind than any other single cause. The true object of religion should be to bind people through love, mutual respect and acceptance so that the mankind can become one large family of God (*vasudhaiva kutumbkam*). People are not saved or unsaved, or redeemed or unredeemed. Life is not a matter of going from evil to good, but from lesser good to higher good, writes Swami Vivekananda (Vivekananda 1963). An individual's life is a spiritual journey to communion with God. On this journey some are just beginning, others have travelled some distance, some have gone farther, while others are near the end of their journey.

A religion is neither true, nor false, but elements of truth and error are present in all religions. 'All faiths constitute a revelation of truth, but all are imperfect and liable to error,' writes Mahatma Gandhi (Attenborough 1982). It is a matter of degree to which a religion has purified itself at a particular time in its history, according to Dr Radhakrishnan (Radhakrishnan 1926).

For a Hindu, religion is a realization that God and man are not separate. Ultimate reality is not accessible to conceptual understanding, but can be directly apprehended in a kind of experience that transcends all names, forms, and concepts.

Chapter 22

The Spiritual Path (*Sadhana*)

> The way to freedom is through service to others. The
> way to happiness is through meditation and being in
> tune with God. Let your heart beat with love for others,
> let your mind feel the needs of others, and let your
> intuition feel the thoughts of others... Forget yourself...
> melt your heart in all, be one with all creation.
>
> Paramahansa Yogananda (Yogananda 1982: 265)

According to Hindu scriptures, that which separates humanity from
God is the mind. That which unites humanity with God is also the
mind. The mind is the cause of both the bondage and liberation of
humanity. The Bhagavad Gita teaches that control of the mind is
essential for spiritual progress, 'Doubtless, the mind is restless and
difficult to control, but it can be brought under control by repeated
practice [of meditation] and dispassion. Just as the wind carries away a
boat upon the waters, the uncontrolled and wandering senses carry
away the wisdom of the mind.' (BG 2,67 and 6,35) Understanding the
nature of one's own mind is thus crucial to every seeker after truth.

An ordinary mind is the consciousness of individuality. Maya (see
Chapter 21) creates this consciousness as the creative power of the
absolute. The core of human life is the self-luminous atman, which
resides in the heart of every human being. The reflected light of the
atman impinges on the brain and gives rise to the mind. Thus the
relationship of the brain and the mind is that of the water and ice. The
brain is the solidified form of the mind, just as ice is the solidified form
of water. Through the mind and body, the unmanifest becomes
manifest in the physical world. If atman is compared to a bird, mind
and the body are its two wings. In the ultimate analysis, the atman,
mind and body are all made of one universal substance, called
brahman by the seers of the Upanishads.

Hindu scriptures maintain that the human mind does not have an
independent existence apart from the atman, the ultimate core of the

human personality. Just as the moon has no light of its own, but shines with the light of the sun, the mind has no light (i.e. intelligence) of its own, but shines with the light of the atman. The relationship of the mind and atman is best illustrated by the chariot metaphor in the *Katha Upanishad*, a Hindu scripture. In this metaphor a person is compared to a chariot where atman is the rider, body the chariot, mind holding the reins is the driver, and senses are the horses. When people lack discrimination and their senses are undisciplined, they are pulled in different directions just as a chariot is pulled in different directions by unruly horses yoked to it. A person who has sound understanding and whose mind is steady is akin to a driver who fully controls the horses of a chariot by reins and reaches the end of the journey.

According to the Yoga Sutras, the mind *(chittam)* includes three faculties or modes of operation. When it is in the mode of thinking and willing, it is called *chitta*. When it discriminates and makes decisions, it is called *buddhi* (intellect). When it claims ownership of human personality and its actions, it is known as *ahamkara* (ego), and when it receives, stores and transmits sensual data, it is known as *manas* (recording, storage and retrieval of information). Yogis tell us that the mind resides in *anahata chakra* (in the heart) during deep sleep, in *vishuddha chakra* (in the neck) during dream state, and in the *ajna chakre* (between the eyebrows) during the waking state. This is why during deep thinking we occasionally holds finger in our chin, turn the neck to the right, transfer our mental gaze towards the space between the two eyebrows, and then begin to think seriously on the problem in hand, explains Swami Sivananda (Sivananda 1997).

The mind dictates the flow of ordinary life. It operates in two modes; one is discriminative and the other imaginative. In its discriminative mode, the mind learns to perceive unity in diversity and leads itself to self-knowledge. The real is one, but the ordinary mind cannot transcend duality and thus makes one appear as many. As long as the mind perceives diversity, it cannot perceive unity. The mind must endure the observed dualities with discrimination. Just as servants can control a weak master, a weak mind can be enslaved by the senses. In its mode of imagination, the mind binds itself to the senses and to the sensual world. The mind of a common person is normally focused on worldly objects, thus the mind's energy is consumed in the senses. A spiritual man turns his mind inwards and directs its spiritual energy towards self-knowledge. Sri Ramakrishna teaches 'Unless one gets rid of egotism, one cannot look for the wisdom of life. Then shall I be free, when I shall cease to be. "I" and "mine" are ignorance. "Thou" and

"Thine" is knowledge.' (Nikhilananda 1977)

Sages and saints inform us that the biggest obstacle to spiritual awakening is the age-old notion of 'I am the body and mind.' This notion derives entirely from the conditioning we receive from our culture from the childhood. Because of this conditioning we remain convinced that we are the bodies having consciousness. Actually we are pure consciousness, which possesses millions of forms (including the human forms), which are continuously created and destroyed as a part of the total phenomena and its functioning. The notion of 'I am the body and mind' as a separate entity is the original sin, says Ramana Maharshi. Saints and seers remind us that to attain perfection in this very life, a quiet mind is all we need. 'Be still and know you are God' is also taught to Christians. Restlessness of the mind is the biggest obstacle for any spiritual experience. Ordinarily when we try to concentrate the mind in meditation or worship, it wanders all over. Arjuna had the same problem when Sri Krishna taught him the philosophy of yoga in the Bhagavad Gita. Arjuna complained that it seemed easier to control the moving wind than to control the mind. Sri Krishna replied that though the mind is restless and hard to control, it can be brought under control by regular practice (*abhyasa*) and dispassion (*vairagya*) (BG 6, 35).

Just as we do not eat the same food, wear same clothes, or drive the same car, so also we do not use the same spiritual discipline (*sadhana*) for self-realization. There are various spiritual paths and the suitability of a particular discipline depends upon many factors, such as the mental attitude, inherent tendencies (*samskaras*), past karma, initial preparation, training and experience, and one's social and cultural environment. All spiritual paths have the same aim that is to realize one's higher self.

There are two major difficulties we normally encounter when we begin to search for a spiritual path. First, we do not fully understand our inner desires and motivations. The reason for this difficulty is that we are taught from childhood how to observe, examine and study the outer world, but we are not taught how to analyze our own thoughts, feelings, ambitions and aspirations. An ordinary mind is not trained to think without an object, yet it is the object-free thinking that reveals our inner desires and motivations. To study the world within, one has to learn how to sit still and regulate breathing so that the mind can penetrate the world within. Yogis tell us that breathing directly affects the mind. Deep and slow breathing calms the mind, whereas shallow and fast breathing excites the mind. The second difficulty is that our minds are preoccupied by superstitions and contaminated with religious dogmas, rites and rituals. Emptying the mind is essential for spiritual growth as is evident from this traditional story:

> A religious scholar approached a Zen Master to learn about Zen teachings. The Master started pouring tea, which soon began overflowing the cup. The scholar shouted, 'Master, Master, the cup is full. It can't hold any more.' The Master replied, 'Yes, like this cup your mind is overflowing with your own ideas. Empty your mind before any more ideas can flow in.'

In western religions, there is no thought of direct experience of higher truth and believers are not allowed to think or search freely about the spiritual dimensions of their own existence.

Spirituality is the science of self-realization and a spiritual path (*sadhana*) can lead to direct experience of higher truth in this lifetime. Spiritual people establish their faith on the path of spirituality with the help of intuition, which is superior to reason. A spiritual path does not prescribe religious rules or rituals, but is a method of examining one's own natural potentials and abilities. A spiritual person can be a religionist, but a religionist is not necessarily a spiritual person. The mind of a religionist is often clouded by the suggestions found in books. The mind of a spiritual person is free, open and ready to investigate and inquire into mysteries of life at all levels: external environment, body, conscious and unconscious states of the mind, and the eternal source of all these modes of life. Fear and ignorance lead to confusion. Fear leads a religionist to fear God, and ignorance leads an atheist to deny God. The ultimate belief in God must be based upon direct experience of the higher reality and that is the primary goal of Hindu spiritual tradition. A spiritual path is a means to this end.

According to Hindu scriptures, *tapas* is the hallmark of a spiritual path. Only a person endowed with *tapas* can be successful on the spiritual path. What is *tapas*? *Tapas* is the restraint of consciousness in the world of space and time and centring of it in itself. *Tapas* is the restraint of senses (not punishment) such that the individual consciousness can redeem itself from the objects of perception and focus on itself.

Choosing the right path for one's spiritual journey is as important as the journey itself. According to Swami Ramdas 'There are two ways to realize Him (atman) – one is to expand the ego to infinity and the other to reduce it to nothing. In both cases, the ego disappears. The former is the path of knowledge, the latter that of devotion." (Ramdas 1994) Although the aim of all *sadhanas* (spiritual disciplines) is the same, the realization of one's higher self, not every *sadhana* is suitable for every person. Therefore, it is important that a seeker prepare himself (or herself) for some time before selecting a particular spiritual path. In the absence of such preparation, there is significant risk of choosing a wrong path. A true spiritual path can become a wrong path if it does not suit the temperament, natural tendencies (*samskars*), the stage of life, and the surrounding individual and family circumstances. The seeker must be physically and emotionally ready to embark on a path. The following guidelines recommended by sages and saints will help any sincere seeker to choose the right path:

- Every human being is a citizen of the two worlds: the outer world and the inner world. Ignoring one and living only in the other cannot lead to a life of fulfilment. The outer world is necessary for one to be a seeker after higher truth and the inner world is the higher truth personified. The outer world demands our full attention to our families and the society. The inner world aspires for love, freedom and peace. For spiritual life, the worldly desires must not be suppressed or repressed, but analyzed. Any suppression or repression of desires creates stress that greatly impacts one's spiritual life. Desires must be analyzed and we must determine which desires create obstacles for ourselves and which desires are helpful. An outward asceticism is not essential, but the conquest of desire and attachment and control over the body and its needs, greeds and instincts are indispensable, writes Sri Aurobindo (Aurobindo 1985).

- Study the lives and works of the great sages and saints and regularly contemplate on their teachings. Study only one book at a time and summarize the teachings after the book is finished. Meditate daily on these teachings for some time before taking on another book. This practice helps to purify the mind and make it ready for the journey. It is said that reading cleans the mind by removing the rust, but it is writing that sharpens it.

- Regularly chant scriptures. Daily chanting of a verse or two from scriptures such as the Bhagavad Gita will expand your spiritual vision and increase your intuition. Ultimately it is the seeker's own intuition that guides towards the right path. Reason, being inferior to intuition, is unable to lead to the right path.

Perform simple yogic exercises regularly to maintain a healthy body. This is needed to house a healthy mind, which is essential for the spiritual life. The difficulty to control the mind is explained by Paramahansa Yoganada, 'You may control a mad elephant; You may shut the mouth of a bear and the tiger; Ride the lion and play with the cobra; By alchemy you may earn your livelihood; You may wander through the universe incognito; Make vassals of the gods; the ever youthful; You may walk on water and live in fire: But control of the mind is better and more difficult.' (Yogananda 1992)

- Meditation is the doorway to intuition. The seeker should meditate regularly for a few years before beginning to search for a path. When seekers are ready, the path will present itself before them. When a seeker is ready for a spiritual guru, their guru will mysteriously appear before them, says Swami Shivananda (Sivananda 1997). What is needed is a sincere effort on the part of the seeker.

- 'Window shopping' is detrimental to spiritual health. Once a path is chosen, sincere effort and patience are crucial for success. Lack of patience pushes the seeker to go 'window shopping'. The result is that the aspirant goes from one path to another thereby wasting time and energy, which results in frustration. Too many modern seekers want quick results without making sincere efforts.

- Timing is critical because if a person begins practising a particular path at a proper time, it is possible to complete the journey in one's lifetime. If the seeker begins too late, when the body has become dysfunctional and the mind has become buried too deep in religious dogmas, practising a particular path may remain a dream only.

The true guru (spiritual master) resides within the heart of every seeker. All one has to do is to learn to listen to one's own heart in the silence of one's own mind. The difficulty is that the mind is normally restless and the ears are plugged with worldliness and thus one cannot hear the inner voice. The above seven steps help to remove the mental restlessness and clean our ears to allow us to hear the inner voice, which is always there to be heard. When the seeker is ready, the inner guru (*atman*) manifests, if necessary, in the form of an outer guru, who then mysteriously shows up in one's life and holds the hands of the seeker.

The need for a guru

Just as a lighted candle is necessary to light another candle, an illumined soul is needed to illumine another soul, says Swami Shivananda (Sivananda 1997). A guru is absolutely necessary for a beginner in the spiritual path, because often the mind is not able to see and correct its own defects and weaknesses. The guru removes doubts and obstacles and leads the disciple in the right direction. The modern slogan, 'think for yourself' does not work on a spiritual path, because human thinking is three-dimensional (see Chapter 19) and cannot lead to self-realization. By service to a guru one develops humility, which is essential for spiritual progress. Service to a guru purifies the mind and renders it fit to receive spiritual knowledge.

In reality, a guru is a principle and not a person. Outwardly a guru will look like a person, a man or a woman, but inwardly he or she represents a principle to which the seeker surrenders to gain spiritual knowledge. Looking upon a guru as a person and judging him or her like anyone else in the world is a spiritual blunder, advises Swami Shivananda (Sivananda 1997). The knowledge gained from books or lectures or by visiting ashrams strengthens the ego and does not lead to self-realization. True knowledge only comes through service to a competent guru, which forces the ego to take the back seat thereby allowing one's attention to shift from the ego to the higher self.

How to choose a guru

Beginners find it difficult to choose a guru, because they do not have the necessary spiritual competence. If they did, they would be so advanced that they would not need a guru. This difficulty is reflected in the often-quoted statement, 'If you can choose a guru, you don't need a guru.' A guru is one who has risen to a higher consciousness and is its manifestation and representative, writes Sri Aurobindo. Such gurus not only help by their example, influence and teachings, but also by the power to communicate their own experience to others. You may take a holy person as your guru if you experience peace in their presence, if they are able to clear your doubts, if they do not disturb your beliefs, but helps you in your *sadhana*, if they are selfless and loving, and if you feel spiritually elevated in their presence, advises Swami Shivananda.

Reason cannot help in selecting a guru, because reason cannot reveal spirituality. The sages tell us that guru and disciple come together in mysterious ways when the disciple has prepared himself and is ready for the guru. The sages advise that once a guru is selected, one must implicitly follow him or her. If you have many gurus, you will be confused, advises Swami Shivananda (Sivananda 1997:155–62). The traditional advice is: 'Listen to all, but follow one. Respect all, but adore one.'

Glossary

Adhikara: spiritual competence, the idea that religious teaching should be graded according to the spiritual competence of the student.

Advaita: monism; non-dualism. Advaita Vedanta expounds the unity of existence and is the most popular school of the Vedanta philosophy.

Agami karma: future karma, which arises through one's present actions.

Ahamkara: literally 'I do'; ego; egoism; I-consciousness.

Ahimsa: non-violence; non-injury; abstinence from injuring any living creature by thought, word, or deed.

Apara Vidya: lower knowledge; the relative knowledge gained through the senses and the intellect that helps in the worldly life, but not in acquiring spiritual knowledge.

Artha: wealth, material possessions; one of the four ends (goals) of the worldly life.

Asana: any of the various bodily postures in Hatha Yoga; a body posture in meditation.

Ashram: a centre for religious study and meditation; one of the four stages of Hindu religious life.

Astral Body: the subtle non-physical body in which the soul leaves the physical body at death on its journey to the astral world.

Atman: individual self, soul, or spirit; the spiritual essence of the individual. In Hinduism the atman is a spiritual reality, which, being eternal, is not created by God. Atman is pure consciousness.

AUM: *see* OM

Avatara: an incarnation of God on earth. An avatara is born as an act of divine will and not as a result of karma.

Avidya: the original ignorance, nescience; the cause of the cosmic illusion that leads to the false perception that the atman (self) is identical with the body and mind.

Bhajana: a song expressing love and devotion for God.

Brahmacharya Ashram: student stage of life; the first of the four stages of Hindu religious life.

Brahman: the cosmic Absolute, the ultimate principle underlying the universe; Supreme Being, Universal Spirit, Ultimate Reality, or Self.

Buddhi: intelligence; the faculty that enables the mind to perceive objects in the phenomenal world.

Chitta: 'mind stuff.' Seat of conscious, subconscious and super-conscious states.

Darshanas: literally 'seeing'. Any one of Hinduism's schools of theology, based upon Upanishads, which are different ways of 'seeing' God.

Deva or **Devta:**   literally 'a shining being'. A divine being or deity.

Dharma: religion; righteousness; the path that one should follow in accordance with one's nature and responsibilities; one of the four ends (goals) of human life.

Dvaita: duality; one of the three schools of the Vedanta philosophy based on dualistic theism, expounded by Madhva.

Gayatri Mantra: the most sacred Vedic mantra in the form of a prayer to the sun for the enlightenment of the intellect.

Grhastha Ashram: the householder stage of life; second of the four stages of Hindu religious life.

Guru: a religious teacher; spiritual guide; a spiritual master who has realized union with God.

Hindu Trinity: The Hindu trinity consists of the three deities of Hinduism, Brahma, Vishnu and Shiva. They are respectively the creator, preserver and dissolver of the universe.

Ishta-Deva or **Ishta-Devita:** a personal god; a chosen deity to whom a devotee offers worship and devotion.

Karma: action (physical, or mental) and its consequence; deeds; results of action.

Kumbha Mela: a sacred Hindu pilgrimage attended by millions of people, making it one of the largest pilgrimage gatherings in the world.

Laws of Manu: a Hindu scripture containing the Hindu social and moral code of conduct.

Lila (or Leela): the divine sport or play of God; Hindus describe creation as the sport of God.

Maharshi: great rishi (seer or sage).

Mantra: 'a mystic formula.' A divine name, sacred syllable, word, or verse used for worship and prayer. Mantras are chanted loudly (or mentally) during *puja* (worship) and religious ceremonies to invoke the divine presence.

Manu Smriti (or Laws of Manu): a Hindu scripture containing the Hindu code of conduct.

Maya: literally 'Deception, illusion, infatuation, appearance'; ignorance or cosmic illusion. According to Advaita philosophy, maya draws a veil over Brahman and also veils our vision and causes humans to perceive the infinite, undivided, and changeless reality (Brahman) as finite, divided, and changing. According to Sankhya philosophy, maya, the inseparable power of Brahman, is the cosmic energy, the material cause of the universe. Maya and Brahman together are called Ishvara, the personal God, who creates, preserves, and dissolves the universe.

Moksha or **Mukti**: final liberation or release from the samsara (the cycle of birth and death); one of the four ends (goals) of human life.

Mukti: *see* moksha.

Namaskara: 'Reverent salutations.' Traditional Hindu greeting where the palms are joined together and held before the heart or raised to the level of the forehead; prostration before a deity, holy person or guru.

Nirguna Brahman: Brahman without attributes; a term used in Vedanta to describe the cosmic Absolute, in its quality-less aspect.

Nirvana: literally 'extinction'; a state of liberation or illumination that frees an individual from the physical limitations (birth and death).

Niyama: ethical observances of Hindus; the second step of Patanjali's Yoga.

OM or AUM: the most sacred symbol in Hinduism. Both by its sound and shape, OM (also called *Pranava*) symbolizes both the personal and the impersonal aspects pf the Supreme Reality. OM is the manifestation of mystic power.

Para Vidya: higher knowledge; spiritual knowledge.

Paramahamsa or **Paramahansa**: literally 'The highest swan'; a title that indicates the highest stage in spiritual development that is union with God.

Prana: literally 'Vital air.' Life breath; vital energy; life principle.

Prasada: the remnants of the food offered to deities during a religious ceremony, which is distributed to all present after the conclusion of the ceremony as a symbol of divine blessing.

Prarabdha Karma: that component of one's past karma, which determines fixed aspects of the present life, such as parents, family, religion, society and one's country.

Puja: a religious ceremony; ceremonial worship of God in the form of a deity.

Purusha: pure consciousness; the term used in Sankhya philosophy to denote the Ultimate Reality; the principle of consciousness as opposed to prakriti, or matter.

Radhaknshnan, Sarvepilli: a philosopher, statesman, and the second President of India (1888–1975).

Ramakrishna: a nineteenth century sage of India, now worshipped by many Hindus as an avatar; the guru of Swami Vivekananda, founder of the Ramakrishna Mission.

Rishi: a seer or a sage. Although there are many rishis noted in Hindu scriptures, the following seven are said to have had the Vedas revealed to them: Gautama (not Buddha), Bharadvaja, Vishvamitra, Jamadagni, Vasishtha, Kashyapa, and Atri.

Rita: literally 'Truth, divine order'; cosmic law; the moral and the natural order in the universe.

Sadhana: a spiritual path or discipline that leads to union with God.

Sadhu: a general term applied to all holy men.

Saguna Brahman: Brahman with attributes; Ishvara; the personal god whom one may worship and adore.

Samadhi: a state of higher consciousness (beyond the waking, dream, and deep sleep states) in which all mental activity ceases; the final stage in yogic discipline in which one attains union with God.

Sampradaya: a Hindu theological tradition; a sect.

Samsara: the world of phenomenal experiences; the phenomenal world in which atman (an individual soul) passes from one life to another, in a perpetual cycle of birth and death.

Samskaras: sacraments; natural impressions and the tendencies of an individual; residual impressions created by karma.

Sanatana Dharma: eternal or universal righteousness; original name of Hinduism.

Sannyasa: renunciation; the fourth and the final stage of Hindu religious life.

Satsanga: company with the holy people or devotees of God.

Self: *see* Brahman

Shaivism or **Shivaism**: one of the three major traditions of worship in Hinduism. The followers of Shaivism worship the Ultimate Reality (Supreme Being) as Lord Shiva.

Shakti: force, power, energy; the consort of Shiva, worshipped as the Divine Mother; the personification of the primal energy of the Lord with which He creates, preserves, and dissolves the universe.

Shaktism or **Tantrism**: one of the three major traditions of worship in Hinduism.

Shankara or **Shankaracharya**: the medieval (788–820) saint and scholar, known as the spiritual genius of India. Shankara was the greatest exponent of the Advaita Vedanta.

Shloka or **Sloka**: a stanza in Sanskrit.

Shuddhi: Purification; a religious ceremony performed to restore Hindu status to anyone who wants to adopt Hinduism including ex-Hindus who may have converted to other religions, but wish to return to their original faith.

Siddhis: supernatural powers; realization; attainment.

Smriti: literally 'that which is remembered'; the secondary scriptures of Hinduism; Hindu religious writings that interpret and/or elaborate upon the teachings of the Vedas.

Srishti: creation; the term is used in reference to development of the universe from its seed state.

Sruti: literally 'that which is heard'; the primary scriptures of Hinduism, the Vedas and the Bhagavad Gita.

Subtle body: the non-physical body in which the soul leaves the physical body at death on its journey to the astral world.

Sukshma sharira: the astral or subtle body.

Swami: literally 'one who is one with the Self'; an initiated member of India's most ancient monastic order; a title of respect and reverence for a spiritual teacher or a holy person.

Trinity: *see* Hindu Trinity

Vaishnavism: one of the three major theological traditions of Hindu religion; worship the Supreme Being in the form of Lord Vishnu and His incarnations.

Varna: literally 'colour' or 'class'; a social class system of the ancient Hindu society.

Varna-Ashram-Dharma: Hindu social system based upon four social classes and four stages (ashrams) of life.

Vasanas: 'subconscious inclinations.' Subconscious thoughts and tendencies; the subliminal inclinations and habit patterns.

Vasudhaiva Kutumbakam: 'all of mankind is one family,' one of the most important doctrines of the Hindu religious tradition, which affirms the unity of existence.

Vedanta: literally 'the end of the Vedas'; the name given to the teachings of the Upanishads and other religious writings that interpret or elaborate upon the teachings of the Upanishads. The *Upanishads, Brahma Sutra,* and *Bhagavad* Gita are the three main pillars of the Vedanta philosophy of Hinduism.

Vivekananda: Swami Vivekananda (1863–1902), the foremost disciple of Paramahamsa Ramakrishna and founder of the Ramakrishna Mission. Vivekananda electrified the American audience by his historic speech on Hinduism in the World Parliament of Religions held in Chicago in September of 1893.

Vrittis: mental activity; thought waves; the waves of mental activities of thought and perception.

Yajna: worship; sacrifice and surrender through acts of worship; a form of ritual worship in which ghee, grains, wood and exotic materials are offered into fire with chanting of mantras in accordance with scriptural injunctions.

Yama: ethical restraints of Hinduism; the first step of Raja Yoga.

Yoga: literally 'union'; a spiritual path that leads to the union with God.

Yogananda, Paramahansa (1895–1952): author of *Autobiography of a Yogi,* one of the most popular books in the world on Indian spirituality. Paramahansa Yogananda taught the science of Kriya Yoga, meditation, and the art of spiritual living in America through lectures, books, and special lessons that he prepared for the dissemination of his teachings. In 1925 he established the Self-Realization Fellowship (SRF) International Organization in Los Angeles, California, from where SRF Lessons are made available to students worldwide.

Works cited

Attenborough, Richard, 1982, *The Words of Gandhi*, Newmarket Press.

Aurobindo, Sri, 1985, *Life Divine* (Vol 1).

Joseph Campbell, 1988, *The Power of Myth with Bill Moyers* (edited by B. Flowers), Doubleday.

Capra, Fritjof, 1984, *The Tao of Physics*, Bantam Books.

Chinmayananda, Swami, 2000, *Talks on Shankara's Vivekachoodamani*, Chinmaya Mission West Pub. Div., Web Site: www.chinmayapublications.org

Chopra, Deepak, 1997, *The Seven Spiritual Laws of Success*, Excel Books.

Dass, Baba Hari, 1997, *Silence Speaks*, Sri Rama Publishing.

Einstein, Albert, 1930, *What I Believe*.

Frydman, Maurice (trans.), 1982, *I Am That: Talks With Sri Nisargadatta Maharaj*, Acorn Press.

Heimann, Betty, 1937, *Indian And Western Philosophy: A study in contrasts*, Allen & Unwin.

Heimann, Betty, 1964, *Facets of Indian Thought*, Schocken Books.

Jawahar, T. R., 2003, Interview with Swami Dayananda Saraswati published on www.newstodaynet.com on June 30.

Krishnananda, Swami, 1995, *Your Questions Answered*, Divine Life Society.

Moody, Raymond, 2001, *Life After Life: The investigation of a phenomenon – survival of bodily death* (revised 25th anniversary edition), Rider.

Moore, Charles A.C. (ed.), 1967, *The Indian Mind*, East-West Press University of Honolulu.

Muktananda, Swami Muktananda, 1978, *A Play of Consciousness*, Harper and Row.

Müller, F. Max, 2000, *India: What Can it Teach us*, Penguin.

Myren, Ann and Dorothy Madison, 1993, *Living at the Source: Yoga teachings of Vivekananda*, Shambala.

Nikhilananda, Swami (trans.), 1977, *The Gospel Of Sri Ramakrishna*, Vivekananda Vedanta Center.

Oldenberg, Herman, 1973, *Grihya-Sutras, Sacred Books of the East,* (Vols. 29–30), Motilal Banarasidas.

Pandit, Bansi, 1997, *Hindu Dharma*, B&V Enterprises.

Pandit, Bansi, 1998, *The Hindu Mind,* B&V Enterprises.

Prabhu, R.K. and U.R. Rao (eds), 1946, *The Mind of Mahatma Gandhi,* Navajivan Trust.

Radhakrishnan, Sarvepalli, 1926, *The Hindu View of Life,* Oxford UP.

Radhakrishnan, Sarvepalli, 1940, *Eastern Religions and Western Thought,* Oxford UP.

Rambo, Lewis, 1998, 'The Psychology of Religious Conversion'; talk delivered at the International Coalition for Religious Freedom Conference on 'Religious Freedom and New Millennium', Berlin, Germany, May 29–32.

Ramdas, Swami, 1994, *God Experience* (2 Vols), Anandashram.

Sivananda, Swami, 1997, *Bliss Divine,* Divine Life Society; Web Site: www.dlshq.org/home.html

Vivekananda, 1963, *The Complete Works of Swami Vivekananda,* Vol. 2, Vivekananda Vedanta Society; Web Site: www.vedantasociety-chicago.org

Vankataraman, T.N., 1984, *Talks with Sri Ramana Maharshi,* Sri Ramanasramam.

Vivekananda, Swami, 1963, *The Complete Works of Swami Vivekanada*, Vols. 2 & 3, Advaita Ashram.

Vivekananda, Swami, 1991, *Chicago Address,* Advaita Ashram.

Yogananda, Paramahansa, 1975, *Whispers From Eternity*, Self-Realization Fellowship.

Yogananda, Paramahansa, 1982, *Man's Eternal Quest,* Self-Realization Fellowship.

Yogananda, Paramahansa, 1992, T*he Divine Romance,* Self-Realization Fellowship.

Bibliography

History and Culture

Alexander George, *The Social Ferments in India* (London: Athlone Press, 1960)

B. B. Lal, *The Earliest Civilization of South Asia* (New Delhi: Aryan Books International, 1997)

D. D. Kosambi, *An Introduction to the Study of Indian History* (Bombay: Popular Book Depot, 1956)

Deo Prakash Sharma, *Harappan Seals, Sealings and Copper Tablets* (New Deli, India: National Museum)

Deo Prakash Sharma, *Harappan Terracottas* (New Deli, India: National Museum)

George Feuerstein, Subhash Kak, and David Frawley, *In Search of the Cradle of Civilization: New Light on Ancient India* (Wheaton, Illinois: Quest Books, 1995)

H. D. Sankalia, *Indian Archeology Today* (New York: Asia publishing House, 1962)

H. D. Sankalia, *The Prehistory and Proto History of India and Pakistan* (Poona: Deccan College, 1974)

L. Basham, *The Wonder That Was India* (London: Sidgwick & Jackson, 1985)

N. S. Rajaram, *Aryan Invasion of India: The Myth and the Truth* (New Delhi: Voice of India, 1993)

R. C. Majumdar (general ed.), *The Vedic Age*, Vol. 1 of *The History and Culture of the Indian People* (HCIP), 4th ed. (Bombay: Bharatiya Vidya Bhavan, 1960)

Shrikant G. Talageri, *The Aryan Invasion Theory: A Reappraisal* (New Delhi: Aditya Prakashan, 1993)

Talageri Srikant, *The Aryan Invasion Theory and Indian Nationalism* (Voice of India Publications, 1993)

V. N. Mishra, *Prehistory and Protohistory* in *Review of Indological Research in Last Seventy-Five Years*, ed. P. J. Chinmulgund and V. V. Mirashi (Poona: Bharatiya Charitrakosha Mandal, 1967)

Religion and Philosophy

Bansi Pandit, *Hindu Dharma* (Glen Ellyn, IL: B&V Enterprises, 1997)

Bansi Pandit, *The Hindu Mind* (Glen Ellyn, IL: B&V Enterprises, 1998)

Betty Heimann, *Facets of Indian Thought* (New York: Schocken Books, 1964)

Betty Heimann, *Indian And Western Philosophy – A study in Contrasts* (London: George Allen & Unwin, 1937)

Brandt Dayton, ed., *Practical Vedanta, Selected Works of Swami Ram Tirtha* (Pennsylvania: Himalayan International Institute, 1978)

Charles A. C. Moore, ed., *The Indian Mind* (Hawaii: East-West Press University of Honolulu, 1967)

Complete Works of Swami Vivekananda (Eight Volumes) (Chicago: Vivekananda Vedanta Society), Web Site: www.vedantasociety-chicago.org/

David Frawley, *Gods, Sages and Kings* (Salt Lake City: Passage Press, 1991)

Deepak Chopra, *The Seven Spiritual Laws of Success* (New Delhi, India: Excel Books,1997)

Donald H. Bishop, *Indian Thought* (New York: John Wiley & Sons)

Encyclopedia of Eastern Philosophy and Religion (Boston: Shambhala, 1989)

George Feuerstein, *The Yoga Tradition: Its History, Literature, Philosophy and Practice* (Prescott, AZ: Hohm Press, 1998)

Herman Oldenberg, *Grihya-Sutras, Sacred Books of he East,* (Vols. 29-30) (Delhi: Motilal Banarasidas, 1973)

Jaideva Singh, *Siva Sutras, The Yoga of Supreme Identity* (Delhi: Motilal Banarasidas, 1979)

Juan Mascaro, *The Bhagavad Gita* (Baltimore: Penguin Books, 1966)

Kenneth W. Morgan, ed., *The Religion of the Hindus* (NY: The Ronald Press Company, 1953)

Klaus K. Klostermaier, *A Survey of Hinduism* (Albany, NY: State University of New York, 1994)

Linda Johnson, *The Complete Idiot's Guide to Hinduism* (Indianapolis, IN: Alpha Books, 2002)

R. S. Nathan, *Symbolism in Hinduism* (Bombay: Central Chinmaya Mission Trust, 1983)

R. V. Pandharipande, *The Eternal Self and the Cycle of Samsara* (Needham Heights, MA: Ginn Press, 1990)

Ralph T. H. Griffith, *Hymns of the Rig Veda* (New Delhi: Munshiram Manoharlal Publishers, 1987)

Ram K. Piparaiya, *Ten Upanishads of Four Vedas* (New Delhi: New Age Books, 2003)

Ray Balli Pandey, *Hindu Samskaras* (New Delhi: Motilal Banarasidas)

Robert E. Hume, *Thirteen Principal Upanishads* (Madras: Oxford University Press, 1958)

Sarvepalli Radhakrishnan and Charles A. Moore, A Sourcebook in Indian Philosophy (Princeton: Princeton University Press, 1973)

Sarvepalli Radhakrishnan, *Eastern Religions and Western Thought* (London: Oxford University Press)

Sarvepalli Radhakrishnan, ed.& tr. *The Principal Upanishads* (London: George Allen and Unwin, 1953)

Sarvepalli Radhakrishnan, *Indian Philosophy* (two volumes) (New York: Humanities Press, 1971)

Sarvepalli Radhakrishnan, *The Hindu View of Life* (London: Oxford University Press)

Satguru Subramuniyaswami, *Dancing With Shiva: Hinduism's Contemporary Catechism* (Concord, CA: Himalayan Academy, 1993)

Swami Chidbhavananda, *The Bhagavad Gita* (Chicago: Vivekananda Vedanta Society, 1997)

Swami Nikhilananda, trs., *The Upanishads* (New York: Bell Publishing Company, 1963)

Swami Prabhavananda & Christopher Isherwood, *Shankara's Crest Jewel of Discrimination (Viveka-Chudamani)* (Hollywood, CA: Vedanta Press)

Swami Rama, *Living With the Himalayan Masters* (Honesdale, PA: Himalayan Institute Press, 1999)

Swami Satchidananda, *The Yoga Sutras of Patanjali* (Yogaville, VA: Integral Yoga Publications, 1990)

Spirituality

Mahendranath Gupta (M), *The Gospel of Sri Ramakrishna* (Chicago: Vivekananda Vedanta Center, 1969)

Maurice Frydman, tr., *I Am That, Talks With Sri Nisargadatta Maharaj* (Durham, NC: Acorn Press, 1982)

Paramahansa Yogananda, *Autobiography of a Yogi* (Los Angeles: Self Realization Fellowship, 1993)

Paramahansa Yogananda, *Man's Eternal Quest* (Los Angeles: Self-Realization Fellowship)

Paramahansa Yogananda, *The Divine Romance* (Los Angeles: Self-Realization Fellowship, 1992)

Ramesh S. Balsekar, *Pointers From Nisargadatta Maharaj* (Durham, NC: Acron Press, 1984)

Self-Realization Fellowship Lessons (Los Angeles: Self Realization Fellowship)

Swami Chinmayananda, *Shankara's Vivekachoodamani.* (Langhorne, PA: Chinmaya Mission, 2000)

Swami Chinmayananda, *Talks on Shankara's Vivekachoodamani* (Langhorne, PA: Chinmaya Mission West Pub. Div.), Web Site: www.chinmaypublications.org

Swami Muktananda, *A Play of Consciousness* (San Francisco: Harper & Row, 1978)

Swami Nikhilananda, The Gospel Of Sri Ramakrishna (Chicago: Vivekananda Vedanta Center, 1977)

Swami Ramdas, *God Experience* (2 Vols.) (South India: Anandashram)

Swami Shivananda, *Bliss Divine* (India: The Divine Life Society, 1997), Web Site: www.dlshq.org/home.html

Swami Sri Ramananda Saraswati, tr., *Tripura Rahasya* (Victor, NY: Ramana Publications, 1959)

Talks With Sri Ramana Maharshi (India: Sri Ramanasramam, 1984)

Miscellaneous

Fritjof Capra, *The Tao of Physics* (New York: Bantam Books, 1984)

Hindu Resources

HINDU UNIVERSE
Web Site: www.hindunet.org/
Hindu Universe, a comprehensive website, provides valuable information on religious, philosophical, cultural, spiritual and historical dimensions of Hinduism.

CHINMAYA MISSION
Web Site: www.chinmayamission.org/
Chinmaya Mission, a worldwide organization, provides excellent educational materials on the wisdom of Vedanta and guidance for spiritual practice.

HINDUISM TODAY
Web Site: www.hinduismtoday.com/
Hinduism Today, a superb quarterly news magazine, provides useful information on all things Hindu.

HINDU UNIVERSITY OF AMERICA
113 N. Econlockhatchee Trail, ORLANDO, FL 32825-3732
Phone: (001) 407-275-0013
E-mail: staff@hindu-university.edu
Web Site: www.hindu-university.edu/
Hindu University of America provides excellent opportunity for learning, research and training in Hindu heritage and the related areas. It includes broad curriculum at baccalaureate, master and doctoral levels in various areas related to Hindu religion, philosophy and culture.

SOUTH ASIA BOOKS
P.O. BOX 502, Columbia, MO 65205
Phone: (001) 573-474-0116
E-mail: sab@socketis.net
South Asia Books is a premier distributor of books from India. It carries a large inventory of books on Hindu religion, culture, history and mysticism.

VEDANTA CENTRE UK
Web Site www.vedantauk.com
Phone: (001) 44-162-852-6464
Email: vedantauk@talk21.com
UK Vedanta centre is a popular institution for study and practice of the Vedanta philosophy of Hinduism. The centre provides guidance for spiritual practice, scriptural reading, and regular discourses on related topics.

WORLD ASSOCIATION OF VEDIC STUDIES (WAVES)
6300 Ackel St. Unit No. 265
Metairie, LA 70003, USA.
Phone: (001) (504) 483-7463
e-mail: bsharma@mail.xula.edu
Web Site: www.hindunet.org/hindu_history/ancient/indus/waves.html
WAVES promotes and supports studies in Vedic tradition including its history, philosophy, science, psychology, literature, linguistic, chronology, ritual, philology, archaeo-astronomy, yoga, and linguistics.

AMERICAN INSTITUTE OF VEDIC STUDIES (AIVS)
PO Box 8357, Santa Fe NM 87504-8357
Ph: 505-983-9385, Fax: 505-982-5807
Web Site: www.vedanet.com/
AIVS is an educational centre for Hindu studies and teaches various related aspects of Vedic Science including Ayurveda, Vedic astrology, Yoga, Tantra, and Vedanta.

NEW AGE BOOKS A-44, Naraina Industrial Area, Phase - I, New Delhi - 110 028, India.
Phone: (001) 2 579 5180, 2 579 2734, 2 579 3423
Email : nab@vsnl.in
Web Site: www.newagebooksindia.com
New Age Books is the best Indian bookstore, which carries over 8,000 titles in 150 subject categories.

HINDU RESOURCES ON LINE
Web Site: www.hindu.org
This website is a resource for information on all aspects of Hindu heritage.

HINDU KIDS UNIVERSE
Web Site: www.hindukids.org/
This web site includes material for children to learn about Hinduism.

Explore Mythology

Bob Trubshaw

Myths are usually thought of as something to do with 'traditional cultures'. The study of such 'traditional' myths emphasises their importance in religion, national identity, hero-figures, understanding the origin of the universe, and predictions of an apocalyptic demise. The academic study of myths has done much to fit these ideas into the preconceived ideas of the relevant academics.

Only in recent years have such long-standing assumptions about myths begun to be questioned, opening up whole new ways of thinking about the way such myths define and structure how a society thinks about itself and the 'real world'.

These new approaches to the study of myth reveal that, to an astonishing extent, modern day thinking is every bit as 'mythological' as the world-views of, say, the Classical Greeks or obscure Polynesian tribes. Politics, religions, science, advertising and the mass media are all deeply implicated in the creation and use of myths.

Explore Mythology provides a lively introduction to the way myths have been studied, together with discussion of some of the most important 'mythic motifs' – such as heroes, national identity, and 'central places' – followed by a discussion of how these ideas permeate modern society. These sometimes contentious and profound ideas are presented in an easily readable style of writing.

ISBN 1 872883 62 1. Published 2003.
Perfect bound. Demi 8vo (215 x 138 mm), 220 + xx pages, 17 line drawings. **£9.95**

Also from Heart of Albion Press

Explore Folklore

Bob Trubshaw

**'A howling success, which plugs
a big and obvious gap'**

Professor Ronald Hutton

There have been fascinating developments in the study of folklore in the last twenty-or-so years, but few books about British folklore and folk customs reflect these exciting new approaches. As a result there is a huge gap between scholarly approaches to folklore studies and 'popular beliefs' about the character and history of British folklore. *Explore Folklore* is the first book to bridge that gap, and to show how much 'folklore' there is in modern day Britain.

Explore Folklore shows there is much more to folklore than morris dancing and fifty-something folksingers! The rituals of 'what we do on our holidays', funerals, stag nights and 'lingerie parties' are all full of 'unselfconscious' folk customs. Indeed, folklore is something that is integral to all our lives – it is so intrinsic we do not think of it as being 'folklore'.

The implicit ideas underlying folk lore and customs are also explored. There might appear to be little in common between people who touch wood for luck (a 'tradition' invented in the last 200 years) and legends about people who believe they have been abducted and subjected to intimate body examinations by aliens. Yet, in their varying ways, these and other 'folk beliefs' reflect the wide spectrum of belief and disbelief in what is easily dismissed as 'superstition'.

Explore Folklore provides a lively introduction to the study of most genres of British folklore, presenting the more contentious and profound ideas in a readily accessible manner.

ISBN 1 872883 60 5. Published 2002.
Perfect bound, demi 8vo (215x138 mm), 200 pages, **£9.95**

Explore Fairy Traditions

Jeremy Harte

We are not alone. In the shadows of our countryside there lives a fairy race, older than humans, and not necessarily friendly to them. For hundreds of years, men and women have told stories about the strange people, beautiful as starlight, fierce as wolves, and heartless as ice. These are not tales for children. They reveal the fairies as a passionate, proud, brutal people.

Explore Fairy Traditions draws on legends, ballads and testimony from throughout Britain and Ireland to reveal what the fairies were really like. It looks at changelings, brownies, demon lovers, the fairy host, and abduction into the Otherworld. Stories and motifs are followed down the centuries to reveal the changing nature of fairy lore, as it was told to famous figures like W.B. Yeats and Sir Walter Scott. All the research is based on primary sources and many errors about fairy tradition are laid to rest.

Jeremy Harte combines folklore scholarship with a lively style to show what the presence of fairies meant to people's lives. Like their human counterparts, the secret people could kill as well as heal. They knew marriage, seduction, rape and divorce; they adored some children and rejected others. If we are frightened of the fairies, it may be because their world offers an uncomfortable mirror of our own.

'*Explore Fairy Traditions* is an excellent introduction to the folklore of fairies, and I would highly recommend it.' Paul Mason *Silver Wheel*

ISBN 1 872883 61 3. Published 2004.
Demi 8vo (215 x 138 mm), 171 + vi pages, 6 line drawings, paperback. **£9.95**

Explore Shamanism

Alby Stone

Shamanism is a complex and confusing subject. There are many different ideas about what shamanism is, who is a shaman, and what a shaman does. *Explore Shamanism* provides a much-needed up-to-date guide to the study of shamanism.

Focusing mainly on the shamans of Siberia and Central Asia, *Explore Shamanism* includes a historical survey of academic approaches to shamanism, an overview of the various theories about shamanism, and a discussion of the origins of shamanism based on the latest ideas. There are also more detailed explorations of the initiation of shamans; the costumes, drums and other tools of the shaman's trade; journeys to the spirit world; and the place of trance, spirit possession and ecstasy in shamanic performance.

Explore Shamanism also surveys revived and reconstructed shamanisms in the world today.

Alby Stone has been studying and writing about shamanism for twenty years.

ISBN 1 872883 68 0. Published 2003.
Perfect bound, Demi 8vo (215 x 138 mm), 184 + x pages, 2 photographs; 17 line drawings, **£9.95**

Also from Heart of Albion Press

Myths of Reality

Simon Danser

'This liberal author's knowledge of
contemporary society is amazingly
broad. He exposits the mythic depths
(and appearances) of everything from
'the myth of science' to superhero
attitudes of contemporary American
nationalism.

'Along the way he challenges many
superficial trivialities about myths
functioning in culture. He regards the
mythic as a primary, highly effective agent of social ideology,
and is never hesitant about demanding that the garments of our
truly mythological capitalism are ill-fitting and socially harmful.

'This is the best book I know in terms of disclosing the
pragmatic functioning of myth in society.'

William Doty, Professor Emeritus, The University of Alabama
and author of
Mythography: The study of myths and rituals

Simon Danser asks us to think of myths as like the lenses in spectacles
– we see the world through them, but rarely see them in their own
right. He then systematically focuses on the myths at the core of the
belief systems which create every aspect of what we take to be reality:
religion, politics, commerce, science, knowledge, consciousness, self-
identity, and much else that we take as 'given'.

This book reveals how reality is culturally constructed in an ever-
continuing process from mythic fragments transmitted by the mass
media and adapted through face-to-face and Internet conversations.

Published by Alternative Albion, an imprint of Heart of Albion Press.
ISBN 1 872883 80 X. 215 x 175 mm, 205 + xiv pages, paperback.
£12.95

Sacred Places:

Prehistory and popular imagination

Bob Trubshaw

Sacred Places asks why certain types of prehistoric places are thought of as sacred, and explores how the physical presence of such sacred sites is less important than what these places signify. So this is not another guide book to sacred places but instead provides a unique and thought-provoking guide to the mental worlds – the mindscapes – in which we have created the idea of prehistoric sacred places.

Recurring throughout this book is the idea that we continually create and re-create our ideas about the past, about landscapes, and the places within those landscapes that we regard as sacred. For example, although such concepts as 'nature', 'landscape', 'countryside', 'rural' and the contrast between profane and sacred are all part of our everyday thinking, in this book Bob Trubshaw shows they are all modern cultural constructions which act as the 'unseen' foundations on which we construct more complex myths about places.

Key chapters look at how earth mysteries, modern paganism and other alternative approaches to sacred places developed in recent decades, and also outline the recent dramatic changes within academic archaeology. Is there now a 'middle way' between academic and alternative approaches which recognises that what we know about the past is far less significant than what we believe about the past?

Bob Trubshaw has been actively involved with academic and alternative approaches to archaeology for most of the last twenty years. In 1996 he founded *At the Edge* magazine to popularise new interpretations of past and place.

ISBN 1 872883 67 2. Published 2005.
275 x 175 mm, 203 + xiv pages, 43 b&w illustrations and 7 line drawings, paperback. **£16.95**

Stonehenge:
Celebration and Subversion

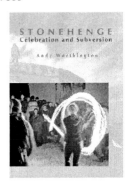

Andy Worthington

This innovative social history looks in detail at how the summer solstice celebrations at Stonehenge have brought together different aspects of British counter-culture to make the monument a 'living temple' and an icon of alternative Britain. The history of the celebrants and counter-cultural leaders is interwoven with the viewpoints of the land-owners, custodians and archaeologists who have generally attempted to impose order on the shifting patterns of these modern-day mythologies.

The story of the Stonehenge summer solstice celebrations begins with the Druid revival of the 18th century and the earliest public gatherings of the 19th and early 20th centuries. In the social upheavals of the 1960s and early 70s, these trailblazers were superseded by the Stonehenge Free Festival. This evolved from a small gathering to an anarchic free state the size of a small city, before its brutal suppression at the Battle of the Beanfield in 1985.

In the aftermath of the Beanfield, the author examines how the political and spiritual aspirations of the free festivals evolved into both the rave scene and the road protest movement, and how the prevailing trends in the counter-culture provided a fertile breeding ground for the development of new Druid groups, the growth of paganism in general, and the adoption of other sacred sites, in particular Stonehenge's gargantuan neighbour at Avebury.

The account is brought up to date with the reopening of Stonehenge on the summer solstice in 2000, the unprecedented crowds drawn by the new access arrangements, and the latest source of conflict, centred on a bitterly-contested road improvement scheme.

ISBN 1 872883 76 1. Published 2004. Perfect bound, 245 x 175 mm, 281 + xviii pages, 147 b&w photos, **£14.95**

Snake Fat and Knotted Threads

An introduction to traditional Finnish healing magic

K.M. Koppana

What did the Finnish cunning man carry in his magic pouch? How does one learn the language of the ravens? What is the Origin of the Cat? How do you attract a partner at Midsummer? These and much more are to be found in *Snake Fat and Knotted Threads*.

Snake Fat and Knotted Threads provides a unique resource about traditional Finnish healing magic and spells, folk customs and myths. All this detailed information is based on the author's research and practical experience.

K.M. Koppana has been interested in spells since she was small, being a keen reader of fairy stories. This interest has persisted and she still has an urge to pick up pebbles on walks. She is also a poet and used to edit small magazines, such as the long-gone *Starlight*, which was about the Finnish magical scene. In 2001 she moved from Helsinki to England, settling in the Midlands.

> *Snake Fat and Knotted Threads* '... is a study of the *tietaja* or cunning folk who used such items as human skulls, graveyard dirt and hangmen's nooses in their magical work. They invoked both the old Finnish gods and Christian deities. This is a highly recommended study of a bygone era of magical belief that in modern Finland has been sadly usurped by New Age therapists and neo-pagan Goddess worship.'
> Michael Howard *The Cauldron*

1st UK edition published 2003 (originally published in Finland). ISBN 1 872883 65 6 Perfect bound, demi 8vo, 112 pages, 14 b&w photos, 2 line drawings. **£7.95**

Heart of Albion

The UK's leading publisher of folklore, mythology and cultural studies.

Further details of all Heart of Albion titles online at
www.hoap.co.uk

All titles available direct from Heart of Albion Press.

Please add £1.30 p&p (UK only; email
albion@indigogroup.co.uk for overseas postage).

To order books or request our current catalogue please contact

Heart of Albion Press

2 Cross Hill Close, Wymeswold
Loughborough, LE12 6UJ

Phone: 01509 880725
Fax: 01509 881715
email: albion@indigogroup.co.uk
Web site: www.hoap.co.uk